Foreign and Female

IMMIGRANT WOMEN IN AMERICA, 1840–1930

REVISED AND EXPANDED EDITION

Doris Weatherford

Facts On File, Inc.

AN INFOBASE HOLDINGS COMPANY

**Foreign and Female: Immigrant Women in America, 1840–1930,
Revised and Expanded Edition**

Copyright © 1995 by Doris Weatherford

  Facts On File, Inc.
  11 Penn Plaza
  New York, NY 10001

Library of Congress Cataloging-in-Publication Data

Weatherford, Doris.
    Foreign and female : immigrant women in America / Doris Weatherford.
      p. cm.
    Includes bibliographical references and index.
    ISBN 0-8160-3100-2 (hardcover)
    ISBN 0-8160-3446-X (paperback)
    1. Women immigrants—United States—Social conditions. 2. Women immigrants—United States—History—19th century. 3. Women immigrants—United States—History—20th century.   I. Title.
    HQ1410.W43 1995
    305.48′8—dc20   95-6685

Text and jacket design by Catherine Rincon Hyman

VB FOF 10 9 8 7 6 5 4 3 2 1

This book is printed on acid-free paper.

Printed in the United States of America

Hitler and His Henchmen

Profiles · in · History

Marylou Morano Kjelle, *Book Editor*

Bruce Glassman, *Vice President*
Bonnie Szumski, *Publisher*
Helen Cothran, *Managing Editor*

GREENHAVEN PRESS
An imprint of Thomson Gale, a part of The Thomson Corporation

THOMSON

GALE

Detroit • New York • San Francisco • San Diego • New Haven, Conn.
Waterville, Maine • London • Munich

© 2005 Thomson Gale, a part of The Thomson Corporation.

Thomson and Star Logo are trademarks and Gale and Greenhaven Press are registered trademarks used herein under license.

For more information, contact
Greenhaven Press
27500 Drake Rd.
Farmington Hills, MI 48331-3535
Or you can visit our Internet site at http://www.gale.com

Cover credit: © USHMM. Adolf Hitler poses with a group of SS (Schutzstaffel) members soon after his appointment as Chancellor.
Library of Congress, 27, 122
National Archives, 107, 135

LIBRARY OF CONGRESS CATALOGING-IN-PUBLICATION DATA

Hitler and his henchmen / Marylou Morano Kjelle, book editor.
    p. cm. — (Profiles in history)
Includes bibliographical references and index.
ISBN 0-7377-1713-0 (lib. : alk. paper)
    1. Hitler, Adolf, 1889–1945. 2. Hitler, Adolf, 1889–1945—Friends and associates—Sources. 3. Nazis—Biography. 4. National socialism—History—Sources. 5. Germany—Politics and government—1939–1945—Sources. 6. World War, 1939–1945—Causes—Sources. I. Kjelle, Marylou Morano. II. Series.
DD253.H526 2005
943.086'092'2—dc22
[B]   2004054142

Printed in the United States of America

Contents

Foreword 7

Introduction 10

Chapter 1: "The Führer"

1. Adolf Hitler: The Early Years
by Jackson J. Spielvogel   24
A failed artist, Hitler found his calling fighting
for Germany during World War I. After the war
he saw the German Workers' Party as a vehicle
to restore his adopted country to its proper place
as a world power.

2. Hitler's First Attempt to Seize Power: The Beer Hall Putsch
by William L. Shirer   36
Hitler's haphazard 1923 plan to overthrow the
government in a Munich beer hall was technically
a failure, but his botched attempt made his name
a household word among the German populace.

3. Hitler's Mission to Exterminate the Jews
by Lucy S. Dawidowicz   52
Throughout his political life, Hitler believed he
was on a messianic mission to annihilate the Jewish people, and he pursued this goal with a
single-minded determination.

Chapter 2: The Elite of the Third Reich

1. Paul Joseph Goebbels: The Little Mouse General
by Louis P. Lochner   61
Paul Joseph Goebbels was a diminutive man who channeled an inferiority complex into the persecution of others while serving as minister of propaganda and public enlightenment.

2. Hermann Göring: Hitler's Chosen Successor
by Douglas M. Kelley   76
Hermann Göring met Hitler when the Nazi Party was in its infancy, and over the years he was appointed, among other titles, Reich marshal and minister of aviation. He was chosen by Hitler to be his second in command.

3. Heinrich Himmler: Mass Murderer
by Joachim C. Fest   90
Heinrich Himmler's flair for organization and his ability to manage small details made him Hitler's choice to oversee the so-called Triangle of Terror: the SS, the Gestapo, and the concentration camps.

4. Rudolf Hess: Hitler's Personal Secretary
by Alfred D. Low   103
As Hitler's "deputy to the Führer," Hess's self-appointed mission of peace to Scotland in 1941 brought him ridicule and imprisonment by the British and a sentence of life in prison at Nuremberg.

Chapter 3: Hitler's Devotees

1. Martin Bormann: The Deputy's Deputy
by Jochen von Lang   114
Martin Bormann came to Hitler's attention by working behind the scenes, eventually rising to

the position of Hitler's secretary. Bormann remained with Hitler in the bunker beneath the Reich Chancellery until the Führer's suicide on April 30, 1945.

2. Albert Speer: Architect and Arms Minister
by John K. Lattimer   129
Albert Speer and Hitler shared a love of architecture. Hitler grew close to his young protégé and eventually made him armaments minister.

3. Ernst Röhm: SA Leader
by Louis L. Snyder   142
Ernst Röhm met Hitler when he was in the process of forming the Nazi Party. Röhm's career as a henchman was cut short when Hitler ordered him liquidated during the "Night of Long Knives" in June 1934.

4. Joachim von Ribbentrop: Hitler's Diplomat
by John K. Lattimer   153
Joachim von Ribbentrop introduced Hitler to the rich and powerful; Hitler rewarded him by making him a foreign ambassador.

Chapter 4: Engineers of Death

1. Rudolf Höss: The Death Dealer
by Roger Manvell and Heinrich Fraenkel   165
Rudolf Höss was made commandant of Auschwitz in 1938. After the war Höss attempted to become anonymous, but in 1946 he was found by the British and turned over to Poland, where he was tried and executed.

2. Josef Mengele: The Angel of Death
by Louis L. Snyder   177
Josef Mengele became a Nazi during the late 1920s, and in 1943 he was appointed chief physician at Auschwitz. He became known as "the

Angel of Death" because of the medical experiments he performed on inmates.

3. Adolf Eichmann: The Embodiment of Evil
by Charles Ashman and Robert J. Wagman   189
Adolf Eichman was head of the Jewish Office of the Gestapo, where he managed the Office for Jewish Emigration. After World War II, he was relentlessly hunted and, after being found in the 1960s, was executed in Israel.

4. Klaus Barbie: The Butcher of Lyons
by UXL   199
Klaus Barbie's loathing of the French made him Hitler's choice to cleanse Lyons of resistance fighters and earned him the title "the Butcher of Lyons."

Appendix of Documents   208
For Further Research   226
Index   231

Foreword

Historians and other scholars have often argued about which forces are most influential in driving the engines of history. A favorite theory in past ages was that powerful supernatural forces—the gods and/or fate—were deciding factors in earthly events. Modern theories, by contrast, have tended to emphasize more natural and less mysterious factors. In the nineteenth century, for example, the great Scottish historian Thomas Carlyle stated, "No great man lives in vain. The history of the world is but the biography of great men." This was the kernel of what came to be known as the "great man" theory of history, the idea that from time to time an unusually gifted, influential man or woman emerges and pushes the course of civilization in a new direction. According to Carlyle:

> Universal History, the history of what man has accomplished in this world, is at bottom the History of the Great Men who have worked here. They were the leaders of men, these great ones; the modelers . . . of whatsoever the general mass of men contrived to do or to attain; all things that we see standing accomplished in the world are properly the outer material result. . . . The soul of the whole world's history, it may justly be considered, were the history of these [persons].

In this view, individuals such as Moses, Buddha, Augustus, Christ, Constantine, Elizabeth I, Thomas Jefferson, Frederick Douglass, Franklin Roosevelt, and Nelson

Mandela accomplished deeds or promoted ideas that sooner or later reshaped human societies in large portions of the globe.

The great man thesis, which was widely popular in the late 1800s and early 1900s, has since been eclipsed by other theories of history. Some scholars accept the "situational" theory. It holds that human leaders and innovators only react to social situations and movements that develop substantially on their own, through random interactions. In this view, Moses achieved fame less because of his unique personal qualities and more because he wisely dealt with the already existing situation of the Hebrews wandering in the desert in search of a new home.

More widely held, however, is a view that in a sense combines the great man and situational theories. Here, major historical periods and political, social, and cultural movements occur when a group of gifted, influential, and like-minded individuals respond to a situation or need over the course of time. In this scenario, Moses is seen as one of a group of prophets who over the course of centuries established important traditions of monotheism; and over time a handful of ambitious, talented pharaohs led ancient Egypt from its emergence as the world's first nation to its great age of conquest and empire. Likewise, the Greek playwrights Sophocles and Euripides, the Elizabethan playwright Shakespeare, and the American playwright Eugene O'Neill all advanced the art of drama, leading it to its present form.

The books in the Profiles in History series chronicle and examine in detail the leading figures in some of history's most important historical periods and movements. Some, like those covering Egypt's leading pharaohs and the most influential U.S. presidents, deal with national leaders guiding a great people through good times and bad. Other volumes in the series examine the leaders of important, constructive social movements, such as those that sought to abolish slavery in the nineteenth century and fought for human rights in the twentieth century. And some, such as the one on Hitler and his henchmen, profile far less constructive, though no less historically important, groups of leaders.

Each book in the series begins with a detailed essay providing crucial background information on the historical period or movement being covered. The main body of the volume consists of a series of shorter essays, each covering an important individual in that period or movement. Where appropriate, two or more essays are devoted to a particularly influential person. Some of the essays provide biographical information; while others, including primary sources by or about the person, focus in on his or her specific deeds, ideas, speeches, or followers. More primary source documents, providing further detail, appear in an appendix, followed by a chronology of events and a thorough, up-to-date bibliography that guides interested readers to further research. Overall, the volumes of the Profiles in History series offer a balanced view of the march of civilization by demonstrating how certain individuals make history and at the same time are products of the deeds and movements of their predecessors.

Introduction

In 1943, when the final European battles of World War II were still more than a year away, the commanders of the Allied forces began planning the postwar destinies of the Nazi leaders. Shortly after Germany surrendered in May 1945, representatives from the governments of the United States, France, the United Kingdom, and the USSR came together in London to draw up an agreement for the prosecution and punishment of the major war criminals of the European Axis. The London Agreement of August 8, 1945, as the document came to be known, set forth in seven articles the legal process by which the Nazis would be tried for war crimes on four counts: the use of government power to plan foreign aggression; the planning and waging of war of aggression; the execution of war crimes (including the murder of civilians and prisoners of war and the wanton destruction of property); and crimes against humanity.

The trials took place in the city of Nuremberg, at the Palace of Justice. The building contained prisons and courtrooms that once served as the military headquarters of the Nazi army and the *Schutzstaffel* (SS), Hitler's elite guard and Nazi police force. The international military tribunal began proceedings in October 1945 before judges from the four major Allied powers. The first trials sought to bring to justice twenty-one of the most prominent and powerful Nazi henchmen, among them party leaders, Reich ministers, military commanders, and representatives of the SS. The tribunal lasted twelve months and focused on vast amounts of testimony and evidence accusing the defendants of the implementation of Nazi atrocities.

As their defense, the Nazi henchmen pleaded ignorance of the scope of their deeds. They claimed they were ordinary citizens merely carrying out the commands of their leader and Führer, Adolf Hitler. They had been used as cogs in a wheel, they maintained, and if anyone was to be held accountable for the Nazi carnage and violence, it should be Hitler.

Hitler himself had taken the only course of action that would ensure he not be brought to trial or brought to justice. On May 1, 1945, as the Allied army was closing in on Berlin, in a bunker far below the Reich chancellery, Hitler committed suicide. In life, Hitler had charged his henchmen with carrying out his disastrous mandates. By his suicide, Hitler abandoned these same close and most trusted supporters, and left it to them to accept both responsibility and consequence. Many of the henchmen paid the ultimate price for being an ardent follower of Hitler, either at their own hands or by hanging in the gallows at Nuremberg.

Hitler's Political Agenda

When Hitler was appointed chancellor of Germany by President Paul von Hindenburg in 1933, he came to the position with a fully prepared political agenda. After failing to be accepted by Vienna's Academy of Fine Arts to study architecture in 1908, Hitler spent the next five years keeping mostly to himself, drawing and selling postcards by day and sleeping in men's shelters at night. Hitler's impoverished lifestyle during his Viennese years became a catalyst for the formation of what he called "a world picture and a philosophy" that became the foundation on which, more than twenty years later, he built the Third Reich. In his own words Hitler explained, "In this period there took shape within me . . . the granite foundation of all my acts. In addition to what I then created, I have had to learn little; and I have had to alter nothing."[1]

In Vienna, Hitler came under the influence of extreme anti-Semites and those who advocated German nationalism through the unification of all German people. Hitler was in agreement with these premises and furthermore believed that a racially advanced group— the Aryans, whom he considered refined and cultured— would establish German superiority. Those who detracted from Germany's attainment of glory—namely the Jews, Gypsies, homosexuals, and others—would have to be eliminated. Hitler became enamored with the possibilities of a strong, racially pure Germany. Less than a decade later, Hitler's passionate love for Germany compelled him to serve as a dispatch runner for the Bavarian infantry in World War I, during which he was injured defending a country to which he did not claim citizenship.

Like his adopted compatriots, Hitler felt the intense humiliation of defeat experienced by Germans at the conclusion of the war and the signing of the Treaty of Versailles. On a national level there was the embarrassment of Germany's crushing financial reparations, the coercion to accept blame for the initiation of the war, and the loss of military might and territory. On a private level, however, Hitler viewed Germany's defeat as a personal affront that reinforced his belief that German greatness could be restored via a strong, racially pure state. To add further fuel to his fire of discontent, Hitler blamed Germany's subjugation on the representatives of the newly formed Weimar Republic who had signed the Treaty of Versailles. He considered these statesmen traitors, called them the "November criminals," and ac-

cused them of stabbing the German army in the back.
The Treaty of Versailles increased Hitler's anti-Semitic feelings. He considered the treaty an obstacle that kept Germany from attaining its rightful presence and glory. That many of the Weimar Republic officials were Marxist Jews provided a focus for Hitler's agenda and reinforced, in his mind, the need for a society free of Jews. He soon began to spread his anti-Semitic propaganda at every opportunity.

Chosen by Providence

Germany's defeat and the punishing Treaty of Versailles furthered Hitler's resolve to restore Germany to its rightful place as a world power. In time, Hitler began to believe that he was divinely chosen to save Germany from Jews and Marxists and preserve it for Aryan magnificence. Hitler's first revelation of divinity came to him after being gassed during the war. According to American psychologist Walter C. Langer, Hitler learned that Germany had surrendered while he was recovering in a hospital from a war injury that had left him temporarily blind and mute. Says Langer,

> [Hitler] had a vision that he would liberate the Germans from their bondage and make Germany great. It was this vision that set him on his present political career and that has had such a determining influence on the course of world events. More than anything else it was this vision that convinced him that he was chosen by Providence and that he had a great mission to perform.[2]

In speeches, Hitler referred to this mission as a "path laid out for me by providence."[3]

After hostilities had ceased, yet while he was still in the army, Hitler's membership in a newly formed right-wing organization called the German Workers' Party (DAP) gave him the opportunity to put his ideology into political practice and earn an income by giving lectures and speeches. On February 24, 1921, Hitler announced the party's "twenty-five points," the bylaws of the organization that he had created with DAP organizer Anton Drexler. These tenets encouraging anti-Semitism and condoning capitalism and democracy became the political foundation of the DAP. By 1921, Hitler had assumed command of the German Workers' Party, now called the National Socialist Party or Nazi Party, for short. The socially inept vagabond who once lived in a Viennese men's shelter found he had a gift of oratory that drew followers by the hundreds. And there was no shortage of disciples from whom to choose the elite that would implement Hitler's political agenda.

Exploiting the Henchmen

National Socialism is synonymous with the name Adolf Hitler. According to Nazi historian Joachim C. Fest in his book *The Face of the Third Reich*, "Any definition of this [Nazi] movement, this ideology, this phenomenon, which did not contain the name Hitler would miss the point."[4] Though Hitler was clearly the driving force behind the Third Reich (it lasted only five days after his death), he did not control the Nazi Party and the Third Reich alone. He stood at the head, but the henchmen who implemented his policies played a large role in Hitler's success. The dictator's inner circle carried out his directives, acted as his advisers on matters of national policy, formulated the means of carrying out his orders, and oversaw their implementation.

Early on, Hitler learned to exploit the attributes of his leaders for personal and party gain. One example of this practice is the case of Ernst Röhm, who was a native of Munich and a captain in the Reichswehr, the German army. Hitler and Röhm became acquainted during the early days of the German Workers' Party. Röhm was a member of the radical right who later used his army connections to secretly provide Hitler and the Nazi Party with weapons and money. Röhm served as Hitler's mentor; he schooled him in the military structure of society that became the trademark of the Nazi state. A flamboyant thug who advocated violence as a means of settling political differences, Röhm was Hitler's choice in 1923 to set up the *Sturmabteilung* (SA), the police force that provided his personal protection in the early days of the Nazi Party.

Hitler shrewdly used his henchmen's various "attributes"—connections, background, violent tendencies, and organizational skills—in delegating responsibilities and creating positions. When Hermann Göring, who would become a reich minister and head of the German air force, was introduced to Hitler in 1922, Hitler was quick to note that Göring's aristocratic background and reputation as a military hero would add credibility to the Nazi Party. Joseph Goebbels's rhetoric and theatrical talents, meanwhile, were put to personal and party use as propaganda minister. Heinrich Himmler, a pedantic individual who could become consumed with the keeping of lists, files, and other minutiae needed to run an organization, was appointed head of the SS. Joachim von Ribbentrop was socially connected through his wife's family's champagne business; this made him a favorable choice to become Hitler's ambassador and foreign minister. Albert Speer demonstrated management abilities beyond his chosen profession, architecture, and became minister of armaments. Hitler's careful selection of his henchmen allowed him to feel confident about the benefits he would receive in return.

Qualities in Common
In addition to the individual background, skills, and personality that brought each henchman to the Führer's at-

tention, many of the elite held core qualities in common. For the most part they were lively and spirited men who directed an enormous amount of energy into fanaticism for the Nazi Party and devotion to Hitler. Many henchmen were educated beyond the *gymnasium*, or high school level; however, they kept their intelligence hidden, for Hitler abhorred intellectuals. Instead, what intelligence the henchmen did have was channeled into bigotry, racism, brutality, violence, and ruthlessness. Hitler's elite could engineer unspeakable atrocities without the slightest sign of remorse, guilt, or shame. Oswald Dutch recorded a prisoner's observations of Himmler in his book *Hitler's Twelve Apostles:* "He looks on indifferently while prisoners are beaten and maimed before his eyes. His only cause for regret is when the victim dies before being able to make a statement which is important to him."[5]

Of all the characteristics required by the henchmen, ruthlessness was the most needed. This became increasingly evident after 1934, when Hitler combined his post as chancellor with that of president and became Germany's "supreme ruler," the Führer. Unopposed, Hitler controlled the fates of millions of people when he ordered the aggressive and brutal directives that led to the Holocaust and World War II. Without the ability to be ruthless, the henchmen could not carry out Hitler's commands, and to not obey the Führer meant the loss of power in the Third Reich. So, to remain in Hitler's favor, his henchmen precisely carried out his mandates.

Hitler oversaw all that was implemented during the years he was in complete control of Germany. He would not tolerate resistance to his authority, nor did he want his henchmen to come up with their own ideas; he wanted complete obedience and compliance with the mandates he put forth. For the most part, the henchmen demonstrated sufficient hunger for power and opportunity to blindly obey their Führer. They did not question their leader, for they had a personal stake in upholding their Nazi oaths to "render unconditional obedience to Adolf Hitler, the Führer of the German Reich, supreme commander of the armed forces."[6]

As Hitler's reign of terror spread throughout Europe and his sphere of influence grew, he depended more and more on his henchmen to carry out his mandates, programs, and plans. And yet he retained supreme control over all of their activities. Guido Knopp in his book *Hitler's Henchmen* states: "Hitler held his Henchmen in a firm grip. They carried out what he decided. Or what in their view was his intention. The killing of the Jews was not the result of the bureaucratic processes of a dictatorship going berserk, but an official crime deliberately staged by Hitler. Hitler not only initiated the killings, he managed them—through powers designated to [Heinrich] Himmler."[7]

The Motives of Hitler's Henchmen

Fest puts forth the theory that there were two types of National Socialists: those who were born National Socialists and those who became National Socialists. Fest cites Joseph Goebbels as an example of someone who became a National Socialist. This type of Nazi, according to Fest, "longed to change existing conditions according to a preconceived ideological plan," and "saw violence and struggle . . . as only the means to carry out this ideological re-education."[8]

On the other hand, according to Fest, there were "born" National Socialists, whom he refers to as "the fighters." These were men such as Röhm, Göring, and Rudolf Hess, another early supporter who would rise to the Nazi Party's number three position. Like Hitler, they had fought in the Great War and were looking for a means of reconciling Germany's humiliation. They also saw the vindication of Germany as a personal quest. Fest writes that they were marked by their war experiences and that "for them, there was now an opportunity extending beyond the war . . . to use their military talents in civilian life, coupled with the promise of power."[9] This confrontational attitude is best summed up by Hermann Göring when he stated, "I joined the party because I was a revolutionary, not because of any ideological nonsense."[10]

Other henchmen's motives for aligning themselves with Hitler were more personal and private than restoring Germany to prewar glory. Many, having had poor relationships with their fathers, were searching for a strong male to serve as their "father figure." This was a role that Hitler, having never bonded with his own father, and having no children of his own, relished. In Hitler, his emotionally needy henchmen found a source for their intense yearnings for affection and approval.

There was no demarcation between the professional and private lives of Hitler's chosen. Hitler infiltrated all aspects. He was the best man at their weddings and godfather to their children, who called him "Uncle Adolf." When Goebbels's marriage was on the brink of dissolution due to his many infidelities, Hitler, who did not tolerate divorce among high-ranking Nazis, acted as a marriage counselor and kept the marriage together. When Hess delayed in asking his longtime paramour, Ilse Prohl, to marry him, Hitler intervened and proposed to her for Hess. Hitler got along well with, and admired, the henchmen's wives, and allowed them to serve as hostesses for Nazi-sponsored functions.

For most of the henchmen, in one way or another, Hitler filled their need for a "savior," a God-like human they could personally worship and publicly obey. Such devotion was not discouraged by the Führer, who believed it to be part of his divine mandate. Not only was

Hitler adored by his henchmen but, with very few exceptions, he was idolized by the general German population as well. The social and political climate in Germany was ripe for Hitler's Messiah complex. His claim to deity is one of the reasons the general population accepted him and looked the other way as the Third Reich boldly implemented its plans for world conquest and mass annihilation. In *The Mind of Adolf Hitler*, Langer writes that Hitler's magnetic charisma extended to German Christians, who proclaimed, "Hitler's word is God's law, the decrees and laws which represent it possess divine authority."[11] And according to Hitler biographer George Victor in his book *Hitler: The Pathology of Evil*, "Many who went to listen [to Hitler speak] with skepticism or even opposition were converted. A new follower said he saw a halo around Hitler's head."[12]

Many henchmen cited Hitler's magnetism in their defense at the Nuremberg trials, and described in detail his hypnotic powers. Hess claimed that the first time he saw Hitler he was overcome by a vision. Speer said Hitler's presence "affected me subtly at our first meeting and from then on never let go of me."[13] And Goebbels wrote to Hitler after their first meeting: "Like a rising star you have appeared before our wondering eyes. You perform miracles to clear our eyes."[14]

As Hitler took on the persona of a redeemer to his elite, so too did the elite become saviors in the eyes of the German populace. According to William Shire in *The Rise and Fall of the Third Reich*,

> In a normal society they surely would have stood out as a grotesque assortment of misfits. Now in the last chaotic days of the Republic they began to appear to millions of befuddled Germans as saviors. . . . They were led by a man who knew exactly what he wanted and they were ruthless enough and opportunist enough to go to any length to help him get it.[15]

A House Divided

Though Hitler's lieutenants were in agreement over their adoration of their leader, they were often at odds with one another. The henchmen ridiculed one another and competed to gain Hitler's favor. Hitler was aware of the combined power of those who were closest to him, and he dealt with the threat by keeping his deputies at odds with one another. He encouraged their bickering and jealousies, realizing that as long as they remained divided among themselves, they would not unite against him. According to Shire, "The Nazi leader was quite content to see strife among his principal subordinates, if only because it was a safeguard against their conspiring together against his leadership."[16]

When Hitler was pleased with his disciples, he rewarded them with additional responsibilities and power, which in turn allowed them to live elegant lifestyles in beautiful homes with plenty of money. When one of the Führer's ideas was not well received, Hitler's followers were quick to make excuses for him, and blamed one another for providing him with incorrect advice.

Just as the henchmen had to be ruthless in order to function in the Third Reich, so was Hitler ruthless when it came to the loyalty he expected from his henchmen. Hitler's own hunger for power was so all-encompassing that any suspicion of treachery against him was dealt with swiftly and mercilessly. On June 30, 1934, the "Night of Long Knives," Hitler ordered the execution of Röhm and others suspected of treason. In the days prior to the end of the war, Göring was ordered liquidated (an order not carried out) when he mistakenly believed that Hitler was summoning him to take over the leadership of the Third Reich. Himmler, in the final days of the war, took it upon himself to try to negotiate peace with a member of the Swedish Red

Cross. When Hitler heard of this, he flew into a rage and ordered Himmler banished from the Nazi Party.

"Clowns or Criminals"?

The men put on trial at Nuremberg were subjected to psychological tests and profiles. The results of these tests demonstrated strong tendencies toward psychopathological personalities as defined by Florence Miale and Michael Selzer in *The Nuremberg Mind: The Psychology of the Nazi Leaders.* These tendencies are antisocial activity with the absence of guilt; highly egocentric feelings; loyalty to hero figures; the idealization of power and success; and the ability to justify and rationalize primitive, aggressive, and egocentric behavior as being in the service of a higher purpose.[17]

Speculation on the psychology of Hitler continues today, nearly sixty years after his death. A painful childhood in a dysfunctional family, the possibility of a Jewish grandfather, a physical deformity, questions about his sexuality, mental illness, and physical illness have all been offered as possible answers to the question of what motivated Hitler to incite, between genocide and war, the deaths of 55 million people.

The Thousand-Year Reich that Hitler and his henchmen had hoped to effect lasted less than five thousand days, yet each and every one of those days had an impact on the world. Going forward into the twenty-first century, historians continue to study the influence of Hitler and his henchmen. Hitler had predicted this would happen in 1920 when he said, "It makes no difference whether they laugh at us or revile us, whether they represent us as clowns or criminals; the main thing is that they mention us, that they concern themselves with us again and again."[18]

Notes

1. Adolf Hitler, *Mein Kampf*, trans. Ralph Manheim. Boston: Houghton Mifflin, 1971, p. 22.

2. Walter C. Langer, *The Mind of Adolf Hitler: The Secret Wartime Report*. New York: BasicBooks, 1972, p. 157.

3. Quoted in Ian Kershaw, *Hitler, 1889–1936 Hubris*. New York: W.W. Norton, 1999, p. 157.

4. Joachim C. Fest, *The Face of the Third Reich: Portraits of the Nazi Leadership*, trans. Michael Bullock. New York: Pantheon, 1970, p. 3.

5. Quoted in Oswald Dutch, *Hitler's Twelve Apostles*. Camden, NJ: Haddon Craftsmen, 1940, p. 111.

6. The Nazi oath of personal allegiance to Adolf Hitler.

7. Guido Knopp, *Hitler's Henchmen*. Phoenix Mill, UK: Sutton, 2000, p. 6.

8. Fest, *The Face of the Third Reich*, p. 72.

9. Fest, *The Face of the Third Reich*, p. 72.

10. Quoted in Fest, *The Face of the Third Reich*, p. 7.

11. Langer, *The Mind of Adolf Hitler*, p. 56.

12. George Victor, *Hitler: The Pathology of Evil*. Washington, DC: Brassey's, 1998, p. 95.

13. Quoted in Knopp, *Hitler's Henchmen*, p. 235.

14. Quoted in Louis Snyder, *Hitler's Elite: Shocking Profiles of the Reich's Most Notorious Henchmen*. New York: Berkeley, 1990, p. 89.

15. William Shire, *The Rise and Fall of the Third Reich: A History of Nazi Germany*. New York: Simon & Schuster, 1981, p. 149.

16. Shire, *The Rise and Fall of the Third Reich*, p. 148.

17. Florence R. Miale and Michael Selzer, *The Nuremberg Mind: The Psychology of the Nazi Leaders*. New York: Quadrangle, 1975, p. 278.

18. Quoted in Kershaw, *Hitler*, p. 147.

Profiles · in · History

"The Führer"

Adolf Hitler: The Early Years

Jackson J. Spielvogel

The appointment of Adolf Hitler as chancellor on January 30, 1933, is considered by many historians to be the act that created Nazi Germany. However, the genesis of Hitler's National Socialist thinking began long before 1933. While he was living in Vienna as a failed artist, Hitler's political views were influenced by German nationalist and anti-Semite scholars such as Georg von Schönerer, Karl Lueger, and Lanz von Liebenfels. Hitler was an enlisted German soldier during World War I, and his love of his adopted country caused him to feel personal humiliation at Germany's defeat. As a result, he was compelled to enter politics in order to work toward restoring Germany's dignity and reputation as a world power. In this excerpt from *Hitler and Nazi Germany*, Jackson J. Spielvogel explores Hitler's evolution from an unknown and unrefined Austrian native to an organizer and leader of the German Workers' Party, the early forerunner of the Nazi Party.

Spielvogel is a historian and associate professor at Pennsylvania State University. His books include *The Essential World History*, volumes 1 and 2, among others.

◆ ◆ ◆

Jackson J. Spielvogel, *Hitler and Nazi Germany: A History*. Upper Saddle River, NJ: Prentice-Hall, 1996. Copyright © 1996 by Pearson Education, Inc. Reproduced by permission.

Adolf Hitler was born on April 20, 1889, in the Austrian village of Braunau-am-Inn, near the Bavarian frontier. His father, Alois, was an Austrian customs official. The Hitler family was of peasant stock, although Alois through his petty bureaucratic position, was the first to break the pattern and enter the lower middle class. Adolf was the fourth child of Alois's third wife Clara Pölzl. There is no real evidence to support the assertion of some that Alois's father and hence Adolf's grandfather was Jewish.

Young Adolf was a willful, indulgent child with strong opinions. His early education was satisfactory, but he was a total failure in the secondary, technical school in the city of Linz, where Alois had settled his family. The family continued to live there after Alois's death in 1903. Claiming illness, Hitler left school in 1905. The real reason was his failing grades. Even in geography and history, which he claimed in his autobiographical *Mein Kampf (My Struggle)* were his "favorite subjects" in which he led his class, he received only mediocre marks.

After dropping out of high school the teenaged Hitler idled away the next two and a half years in Linz, drawing, painting, writing poetry, going to the theater, and daydreaming. In many ways, this period of Hitler's life, especially as revealed by his youthful Linz friend and companion, August Kubizek, foreshadows much of his later life pattern. According to Kubizek, Hitler was a dreamer who preferred creating fantasies to doing any real work. His mania for redesigning and reconstructing cities appears in his grandiose plans for the rebuilding of Linz. As Kubizek related, "the more remote the realization of a project was, the more did he steep himself in it. To him these projects were in every detail as actual as though they were already executed." Hitler believed that one day he would carry out his projects.

According to Kubizek, the young Hitler was impatient, moody, irritable if contradicted, and prone to outbursts of temper. He disdained regular work, preferring to live what he considered the life of the artist. He was a compulsive talker, inclined to giving dramatic speeches in which he was carried away by his own emotions. He was extraordinarily serious: "He approached the problems with which he was concerned with a deadly earnestness which ill suited his sixteen or seventeen years" [according to Kubizek]. Willful and determined, the young Adolf, contrary to his mother's and brother-in-law's wishes, decided to pursue art as his career.

A Failed Artist

In September 1907 Hitler left Linz to go to Vienna, where he applied to the Vienna Academy of Fine Arts. His painting samples were declared unsatisfactory and he was refused admission. The director suggested architecture, but Hitler needed a diploma from secondary school to enroll in a school of architecture. He did not have one and was certainly unwilling to take the final exams to get one. He returned briefly to Linz for his mother's death in December 1907, a deeply emotional experience since [according to Kubizek] "she was the only person on earth to whom he felt really close." In February 1908 he returned to Vienna and remained there until 1913.

Hitler did not recall his Viennese years with any fondness.

> To me Vienna, the city which, to so many, is the epitome of innocent pleasure, a festive playground for merrymakers, represents, I am sorry to say, merely the living memory of the saddest period of my life. Even today this city can arouse in me nothing but the most dismal thoughts. For me the name of this . . . city represents five years of hardship and

misery. Five years in which I was forced to earn a living, first as a day laborer, then as a small painter; a truly meager living which never sufficed to appease even my daily hunger. Hunger was then my faithful bodyguard.

Hitler's account of his great poverty was simply not true. In his first few years in Vienna, Hitler had the benefit of an inheritance from his father, his mother's legacy, and an orphan's pension, all of which probably brought him 80 to 100 crowns a month, equivalent to the earnings of a junior magistrate. Later he inherited a considerable sum from his aunt. Essentially Hitler went to Vienna to escape work and to continue the lifestyle of an artist.

Adolf Hitler

He was joined in Vienna by his friend Kubizek, who enrolled as a music student in the Vienna Conservatory and roomed with Hitler for almost six months. Kubizek has given us an account of how Hitler spent his days in Vienna, frequenting museums and libraries. At night he went to the opera, especially to see the works of Richard Wagner. He saw his favorite, *Lohengrin*, ten times. As in his Linz days, Hitler continued to create fantastic projects. He began an opera, started a play, and drew up detailed architectural plans for the reconstruction of Vienna. When Kubizek asked him one day what he was doing, Hitler responded, "I am working on the solution of the housing problem in Vienna, and I am doing certain research for this purpose; I therefore have to go around a lot."

Kubizek left Vienna in July 1908 for an army stint. When he returned in November planning to room again with Hitler, he discovered that his friend had moved without leaving a forwarding address. From late 1908 to 1913 Hitler's Viennese years were spent in the shadowy world of public shelters and hostels for men. Increasingly, as his early sources of income dried up, Hitler's financial circumstances became more difficult. During these years, Hitler pieced together the fragments of a *Weltanschauung* [world outlook] that he would never change: "In this period there took shape within me a world picture and a philosophy which became the granite foundation of all my acts. In addition to what I then created, I have had to learn little, and I have had to alter nothing" [Hitler wrote]. This world picture was based on the political ideas and movements and the social conflicts of early-twentieth-century Vienna. What were the influences that Hitler experienced there?

Influences on Hitler's Development

In *Mein Kampf*, Hitler refers to two of the political figures who made a significant impact on him, Georg von Schönerer and Karl Lueger. Schönerer was the leader of the Austrian pan-German movement. He was an extreme German nationalist who desired the union of all Germans in one national state and hence opposed the continuing existence of the Austrian multinational state. Schönerer's movement was also anti-Semitic. The rabid pan-German nationalist turned anti-Semitism from a religiously and economically motivated movement to one that was politically and racially oriented. Hitler criticized Schönerer, however, for his inability to understand the "social question," since Schönerer neglected the masses by directing his attention to the middle classes.

Karl Lueger was the mayor of Vienna and leader of the anti-Semitic Christian Social party. Hitler, with his usual lack of moderation, referred to him as "the greatest German mayor of all times" and a "statesman greater than all the so-called diplomats of the time." He especially admired Lueger's demagogic methods, including his ability to use propaganda to appeal to the masses. Hitler believed that Lueger understood the politics of a mass party formed with the aid of emotional slogans. Part of Lueger's appeal lay in his clever manipulation of anti-Semitism, although Hitler felt that Lueger merely used it for political purposes without correctly understanding the racial significance of anti-Semitism. Lueger also failed, in Hitler's eyes, to grasp the significance of German nationalism, since he continued to support the multinational Austrian state. . . .

[Under the influence of Schönerer and Lueger] Hitler established the contours of his own Nazi party. It would be based on a strong German nationalism, socialism (or at least Hitler's version of it in his attempt to win over the masses), and extreme anti-Semitism.

Hitler's attitudes toward anti-Semitism were probably most influenced by an ex-Catholic monk named Adolf Lanz who called himself Lanz von Liebenfels. Liebenfels founded the quasi-religious Order of the New Templars, whose primary purpose was to foster Ariosophical doctrines. Ariosophy was a combination of occult ideas, German *völkisch* nationalism, and anti-Semitism. . . . [According to Liebenfels] Jews, as well as other allegedly inferior races, were characterized as "animal-men" who must someday be eliminated by genetic selection, sterilization, deportations, forced labor, and even "direct liquidation." The elimination of the "animal-man" made possible the coming of the "higher new man," the Aryan superhero. . . .

One cannot discuss influences on the ideas of the early Hitler without stressing the importance of Richard Wagner. . . . [Hitler] was . . . influenced by the composer's life and political ideas and later claimed that he had no forerunners except Richard Wagner. One of Wagner's appeals to the young Hitler was the myth of the outsider, who follows his own rhythms and is forced to oppose the straitlaced social order of his day determined by tradition. In Wagner's *Rienzi* and *Lohengrin* Hitler could see aspects of his own rejection by the world. The need to dominate is also an underlying theme in much of Wagner's music, and from this urge came Hitler's attempts to overwhelm through imposing demonstrations of power. The later public ceremonies of the Third Reich, with their massive stage effects, owe much to the influence of Wagner's operas on Hitler.

The Need for Struggle

If his time in Vienna was the formative period of Hitler's world picture and philosophy, what then were the basic ideas that he had absorbed and made into an ideology that he would adhere to for the rest of his life? Racial anti-Semitism was clearly at the core of his ideas. Moreover, Hitler had become an extreme German nationalist who favored the union of all German peoples. Anti-Semitism and nationalism were, of course, stock ideas in the bourgeois world of both Linz and Vienna. Viennese mass politics gave Hitler practical examples of the effective use of propaganda and terror by political parties. Finally, underlying all of his beliefs was a strong conviction of the need for struggle. The world was a brutal place filled with a constant struggle for existence in which only the fit survived. . . .

Hitler's years in Vienna served as the foundation for his later experiences. Here he developed an ideology from which he did not deviate for the rest of his life. He had the conviction of the closed-minded fanatic who sees no need to pursue new ideas in response to new situations. Adolf Hitler never doubted that the world could be seen in only one way—his way. Vienna had been a time of despair because of his frustration in not being recognized as the great artist and genius that he believed himself to be. The rejected Hitler projected his anger and hatred against the Jews, the bourgeois world, the rich, the aristocrats. He could blame everyone for his personal disasters except the one person actually responsible—himself. Adolf Hitler left Vienna in 1913 with no real purpose, hating a world that had rejected him but convinced that he would someday be recognized.

Hitler, the Soldier

In May 1913 Hitler moved to Munich. He claimed that he had made the move because of his passionate aversion to the Austrian Empire and his longing for the art capital of Bavaria. His real reason was to escape Austrian military obligations. Although the authorities caught up with the draft dodger, he was rejected as physically unfit for military service.

Munich brought no real change to Hitler's life. He continued to sell his paintings to keep alive. The escape from Vienna and the move to Germany had solved nothing. He had no real future in sight. The outbreak of World War I proved to be his salvation: "To me these hours seemed like a release from the painful feeling of my youth. . . . Overpowered by stormy enthusiasm, I fell down on my knees and thanked Heaven from an overflowing heart for granting me the good fortune of being permitted to live at this time" [wrote Hitler]. Hitler volunteered for the Bavarian army and was accepted on August 3, 1914. At the age of twenty-five, Adolf Hitler had at last found a purpose for his life. The formerly undisciplined bohemian now accepted a grueling regimen for the sake of serving a greater purpose, Germany's greatness. Hitler threw himself into the war with great energy. As a dispatch runner, he distinguished himself by his courageous acts and received the Iron Cross, First Class, seldom awarded to enlisted men. He was, however, promoted only to corporal. His dedicated patriotism and willingness to sacrifice his personal interests for higher ideals made him unattractive to his fellow soldiers. A loner who shunned common vices, Hitler simply did not fit in with the other soldiers. But the military with its clear-cut system of order and values and its sense of male camaraderie made a great impact on Hitler's later lifestyle. So, too, did the excitement and discipline of war.

The news of Germany's defeat, which he heard while being treated at a military hospital for temporary blindness from a gas attack at the front, touched Hitler to the core of his being. Although he grieved for Germany, his own newfound existence was also jeopardized. The war had brought purpose and meaning to his life. He could not return to his wretched prewar condition. To Hitler, the war could not have been lost by the army. Defeat had been caused by the weakness of the home front; the army had suffered a Jewish-Marxist "stab in the back." As a result of a vision he claimed to have had while blinded, he decided early in November 1918 that he would go into politics to redress these dreadful wrongs.

Hitler Enters Politics

Upon his return to Munich, Hitler did little at first to transform his vision into reality. He remained in the army during the postwar turmoil in Munich that saw the temporary establishment of the Soviet Republic in April 1919. Hitler's German nationalistic enthusiasm led his superiors to appoint him an information officer who could indoctrinate his fellow soldiers with German ideals. His job also entailed observation of small right-wing parties that might ultimately be of assistance to the German army. On one occasion, in September 1919,

Hitler wound up in a Munich beer hall as an observer at a meeting of one such right-wing party, the German Workers' party (DAP). It turned out to be Hitler's entry into politics.

The German Workers' party was merely one of many right-wing *völkisch*-nationalist parties in Munich. The Bavarian capital was especially conducive to extreme right-wing politics. In 1919 the army and Free Corps groups had crushed the Soviet Republic and reestablished the moderate Socialist government in Bavaria. But in 1920 . . . a coup replaced the Socialist government with a right-wing regime under the conservative Gustav von Khar. Because the Weimar constitution granted control of the police to the governments of the individual federal states rather than to the central government, the Bavarian rightist regime provided a haven for the extremist activities of right-wing *völkisch*-nationalist groups. One of the most important of these groups was the Thule Society. . . .

The Thule Society essentially combined occult racial philosophy (in the tradition of Lanz von Liebenfels) with a belief in militant action. The Thule Society preached Aryan supremacy and acted to achieve it. Although the society functioned outwardly as a "German studies" group, it was actively involved in the counterrevolution against the Bavarian Soviet Republic, which the Thule Society felt was dominated by Jews. . . .

The German Workers' Party

The German Workers' party, which Hitler joined and later renamed, was found by the railway mechanic Anton Drexler early in 1919 under the chairmanship of Karl Harrer, a journalist and member of the Thule. In fact, the German Workers' party had a number of close links with the Thule Society. Hitler also had intimate ties with Thule members. Dietrich Eckart, whom

Hitler accepted as his mentor and praised as the father of the Nazi movement, Alfred Rosenberg, eventually the Nazi party's ideologist, and Rudolf Hess, Hitler's future second-in-command, were all members of the Thule Society.

In *Mein Kampf*, Hitler gave his own version of his relationship with the German Workers' party. After attending a meeting at which [an early party executive] Gottfried Feder spoke on finance capital and the elimination of capitalism, Hitler was prevailed upon to join the party as member number fifty-five and at the same time member seven of the executive committee. This small party of mediocrities gave Hitler an outlet for his own political interests and especially an opportunity to play a leading role. As propaganda chairman of the party, Hitler was able to develop his organizational skills, but above all to discover his oratorical talents. A month after joining the party, as a result of his first major speech, on October 16, 1919, he found that he "could speak." Thereafter, he spoke regularly at DAP gatherings as well as to other *völkisch* groups outside of Munich. From his position on the executive committee, Hitler began to gradually change the DAP from a mere discussion group to a noisy, publicity-seeking party of struggle, a mass political party.

The Twenty-Five Points

On February 24, 1920, the German Workers' party held its first authentic mass meeting in the Hofbräuhaus, a large Munich beer cellar. Hitler was overjoyed by the attendance of almost 2000 people and used the opportunity to announce a twenty-five-point party program composed by himself and Drexler. The program made clear that the new movement opposed capitalism, democracy, and especially the Jews. The latter were, in fact, to be excluded from German citizenship

(point 4: "No Jew can be a member of the nation").
The party program was strongly nationalistic and im-
perialistic (point 1: "We demand the union of all Germans in a Greater Germany upon the basis of the self-
determination of the people"; point 3: "We demand
land and territory [colonies] for the nourishment of our
people and for settling our excess population"). The influence of Hitler on the party program was evident in
the call for the revocation of the Treaty of Versailles
and the stress on the unalterable nature of the program.
Both the party program and Hitler's early speeches
provided simple explanations for the German misery:
the Jews, Marxists, the Versailles treaty, and the "November criminals"—the democratic leaders who had
stabbed the army in the back [by signing the armistice
ending World War I].

In Hitler's eyes, the Hofbräuhaus mass meeting was
a turning point for the new movement: "By it the party
burst the narrow bonds of a small club and for the first
time exerted a determining influence on the mightiest
factor of our time, public opinion." The party's name
was changed to the National Socialist German Workers' Party (NSDAP), or Nazi for short, to distinguish
itself from the socialist parties while gaining support
from working-class and *völkisch*-nationalist circles alike.
In April 1920 Hitler took the decisive step of quitting
the army and dedicating himself completely to politics.
It was a logical step. Politics proved to be the ideal vocation for one who had no vocation and was certainly
not trained for any. The Nazi movement had begun.

Hitler's First Attempt to Seize Power: The Beer Hall Putsch

William L. Shirer

Post–World War I Germany was chaotic. Crushed by military defeat and humiliated by the terms of the Treaty of Versailles, which placed responsibility for the war on Germany, the German populace was besieged daily by new political parties rising in protest against Germany's new government, the Weimar Republic. One such group, the Nazis, headed by a fiery rebel named Adolf Hitler, attempted a takeover of the Bavarian government in Munich in 1923. In this selection from *The Rise and Fall of the Third Reich: A History of Nazi Germany*, William L. Shirer describes Hitler's first attempt at a government takeover as ill conceived and lacking in contingency. Shirer also shows Hitler as a man who, when met with resistance, chose to escape to safety rather than face danger.

Shirer worked as a broadcaster in Europe in the years leading up to World War II. During the war he worked as a correspondent, reporting on the German army from its positions on the battlefield.

William L. Shirer, *The Rise and Fall of the Third Reich: A History of Nazi Germany*. New York: Simon & Schuster, 1960. Copyright © 1959 by William L. Shirer. All rights reserved. Reproduced by permission of Simon & Schuster Adult Publishing Group.

The hardships and uncertainties of the wanton inflation [under the Weimar government] were driving millions of Germans toward [the] conclusion [that dictatorship would be preferable] and Hitler was ready to lead them on. In fact, he had begun to believe that the chaotic [political, social, and economic] conditions of 1923 had created an opportunity to overthrow the Republic which might not recur. But certain difficulties lay in his way if he were himself to lead the counterrevolution, and he was not much interested in it unless he was.

In the first place, the Nazi Party, though it was growing daily in numbers, was far from being even the most important political movement in [the German state of] Bavaria, and outside that state it was unknown. How could such a small party overthrow the Republic [the Weimar government established after World War I]? Hitler, who was not easily discouraged by odds against him, thought he saw a way. He might unite under his leadership all the antirepublican, nationalist forces in Bavaria. Then with the support of the Bavarian government, the armed leagues and the Reichswehr [government armed guards] stationed in Bavaria, he might lead a march on Berlin—as [Italian dictator Benito] Mussolini had marched on Rome the year before—and bring the Weimar Republic down. Obviously Mussolini's easy success had given him food for thought.

The French occupation of the Ruhr [in 1922], though it brought a renewal of German hatred for the traditional enemy and thus revived the spirit of nationalism, complicated Hitler's task. It began to unify the German people behind the republican government in Berlin which had chosen to defy France. This was the last thing Hitler wanted. His aim was to do away with the Republic. France could be taken care of after Germany had had its nationalist revolution and established a dictatorship. Against a strong current of public opinion Hitler dared to take an unpopular line: "No—not down with France, but down with the traitors of the Fatherland, down with the November criminals [the German leaders who signed the armistice ending World War I]! That must be our slogan."

All through the first months of 1923 Hitler dedicated himself to making the slogan effective. In February, due largely to the organizational talents of [Ernst] Roehm [one of the original organizers of the Nazi Party and head of the Sturmabteilung (S.A.)] four of the armed "patriotic leagues" of Bavaria joined with the Nazis to form the so-called Arbeitsgemeinschaft der Vaterlaendischen Kampfverbaende (Working Union of the Fatherland Fighting Leagues) under the political leadership of Hitler. In September an even stronger group was established under the name of the Deutscher Kampfbund (German Fighting Union), with Hitler one of a triumvirate of leaders. This organization sprang from a great mass meeting held at Nuremberg on September 2 to celebrate the anniversary of the German defeat of France at Sedan in 1870. Most of the fascist-minded groups in southern Germany were represented and Hitler received something of an ovation after a violent speech against the national government. The objectives of the new Kampfbund were openly stated: overthrow of the Republic and the tearing up of the Treaty of Versailles.

At the Nuremberg meeting Hitler had stood in the reviewing stand next to General [Erich] Ludendorff during a parade of the demonstrators. This was not by accident. For some time the young Nazi chief had been cultivating the war hero, who had lent his famous name to the makers of the Kapp putsch in Berlin and who, since he continued to encourage counterrevolution from the Right, might be tempted to back an action which was beginning to germinate in Hitler's mind. . . . [Hitler] did not want Ludendorff as the political leader of the nationalist counterrevolution, a role which it was known the war hero was ambitious to assume. Hitler insisted on that role for himself. But Ludendorff's name, his renown in the officer corps and among the conservatives throughout Germany would be an asset to a provincial politician still largely unknown outside Bavaria. Hitler began to include Ludendorff in plans.

Crisis in Bavaria

In the fall of 1923 the German Republic and the state of Bavaria reached a point of crisis. On September 26, Gustav Stresemann the [German] Chancellor, announced the end of passive resistance in the Ruhr and the resumption of German reparation payments. This former mouthpiece of [Paul von] Hindenburg and Ludendorff, a staunch conservative and, at heart, a monarchist, had come to the conclusion that if Germany were to be saved, united and made strong again it must, at least for the time being, accept the Republic, come to terms with the Allies and obtain a period of tranquillity in which to regain its economic strength. To drift any further would only end in civil war and perhaps in the final destruction of the nation.

The abandonment of resistance to the French in the Ruhr and the resumption of the burden of reparations touched off an outburst of anger and hysteria among the German nationalists, and the Communists, who also had been growing in strength, joined them in bitter denunciation of the Republic. . . .

Bavaria remained defiant of Berlin. It was now under the dictatorial control of a triumvirate: Kahr, the State

Commissioner, General Otto von Lossow, commander
of the Reichswehr in Bavaria, and Colonel Hans von
Seisser, the head of the state police. . . . [Kahr] declined
to carry out an order from Berlin. . . .

This, to Berlin, was not only political but military re-
bellion, and General von Seeckt was now determined
to put down both.

He issued a plain warning to the Bavarian triumvirate and to Hitler and the armed leagues that any re-
bellion on their part would be opposed by force. But for
the Nazi leader it was too late to draw back. His rabid
followers were demanding action. Lieutenant Wilhelm
Brueckner, one of his S.A. commanders, urged him to
strike at once. "The day is coming," he warned, "when
I won't be able to hold the men back. If nothing hap-
pens now, they'll run away from us."

Hitler Plans the Putsch

Hitler realized too that if Stresemann gained much more
time and began to succeed in his endeavor to restore
tranquillity in the country, his own opportunity would be
lost. He pleaded with Kahr and Lossow to march on
Berlin before Berlin marched on Munich. And his suspicion grew that either the triumvirate was losing heart or
that it was planning a separatist coup without him for the
purpose of detaching Bavaria from the Reich. To this,
Hitler, with his fanatical ideas for a strong, nationalist,
unified Reich, was unalterably opposed.

Kahr, Lossow and Seisser were beginning to lose
heart after Seeckt's warning. They were not interested
in a futile gesture that might destroy them. On November 6 they informed the Kampfbund, of which
Hitler was the leading political figure, that they would
not be hurried into precipitate action and that they
alone would decide when and how to act. This was a
signal to Hitler that he must seize the initiative himself.

He did not possess the backing to carry out a putsch alone. He would have to have the support of the Bavarian state, the Army and the police—this was a lesson he had learned in his beggarly Vienna days. Somehow he would have to put Kahr, Lossow and Seisser in a position where they would have to act with him and from which there would be no turning back. Boldness, even recklessness, was called for, and that Hitler now proved he had. He decided to kidnap the triumvirate and force them to use their power at his bidding. . . .

A brief notice appeared in the press that, at the request of some business organizations in Munich, Kahr would address a meeting at the Buergerbräukeller, a large beer hall on the southeastern outskirts of the city. The date was November 8, in the evening. The subject of the Commissioner's speech, the notice said, would be the program of the Bavarian government. General von Lossow, Colonel von Seisser and other notables would be present.

Two considerations led Hitler to a rash decision. The first was that he suspected Kahr might use the meeting to announce the proclamation of Bavarian independence and the restoration of the Wittelsbachs to the Bavarian throne. All day long on November 8 Hitler tried in vain to see Kahr, who put him off until the ninth. This only increased the Nazi leader's suspicions. He must forestall Kahr. . . . Hitler decided to act at once. . . . The storm troops were hastily alerted for duty at the big beer hall.

The Beer Hall Putsch

About a quarter to nine on the evening of November 8, 1923, after Kahr had been speaking for half an hour to some three thousand thirsty burghers, seated at rough-hewn tables and quaffing their beer out of stone mugs in the Bavarian fashion, S.A. troops surrounded the Buergerbräukeller and Hitler pushed forward into the hall. While some of his men were mounting a machine gun in the entrance, Hitler jumped up on a table and to attract attention fired a revolver shot toward the ceiling. Kahr paused in his discourse. The audience turned around to see what was the cause of the disturbance. Hitler, with the help of Hess and of Ulrich Graf, the former butcher, amateur wrestler and brawler and now the leader's bodyguard, made his way to the platform. A police major tried to stop him, but Hitler pointed his pistol at him and pushed on. Kahr, according to one eyewitness, had now become "pale and confused." He stepped back from the rostrum and Hitler took his place.

"The National Revolution has begun!" Hitler shouted. "This building is occupied by six hundred heavily armed men. No one may leave the hall. Unless there is immediate quiet I shall have a machine gun posted in the gallery. The Bavarian and Reich governments have been removed and a provisional national government formed. The barracks of the Reichswehr and police are occupied. The Army and the police are marching on the city under the swastika banner."

This last was false; it was pure bluff. But in the confusion no one knew for sure. Hitler's revolver was real. It had gone off. The storm troopers with their rifles and machine guns were real. Hitler now ordered Kahr, Lossow and Seisser to follow him to a nearby private room off stage. Prodded by storm troopers, the three highest officials of Bavaria did Hitler's bidding while the crowd looked on in amazement.

But with growing resentment too. Many businessmen still regarded Hitler as something of an upstart. One of them shouted to the police, "Don't be cowards as in 1918. Shoot!" But the police, with their own chiefs so docile and the S.A. taking over the hall, did not budge. Hitler had arranged for a Nazi spy at police headquarters, Wilhelm Frick, to telephone the police on duty at the beer hall not to interfere but merely to report. The crowd began to grow so sullen that [Hermann] Goering felt it necessary to step to the rostrum and quiet them. "There is nothing to fear," he cried. "We have the friendliest intentions. For that matter, you've no cause to grumble, you've got your beer!" And he informed them that in the next room a new government was being formed.

It was, at the point of Adolf Hitler's revolver. Once he had herded his prisoners into the adjoining room, Hitler told them, "No one leaves this room alive without my permission." He then informed them they would all have key jobs either in the Bavarian government or in the Reich government which he was forming with Ludendorff. With Ludendorff? Earlier in the evening Hitler had dispatched [Max Erwin von] Scheubner-Richter [a Russian refugee and coconspirator of Hitler's] to Ludwigshoehe to fetch the renowned General, who knew nothing of the Nazi conspiracy, to the beerhouse at once.

The three prisoners at first refused even to speak to Hitler. He continued to harangue them. Each of them must join him in proclaiming the revolution and the new governments; each must take the post he, Hitler, assigned them, or "he has no right to exist." Kahr was to be the Regent of Bavaria; Lossow, Minister of the National Army; Seisser, Minister of the Reich Police. None of the three was impressed at the prospect of such high office. They did not answer. . . .

Hitler Announces Victory

[Hitler] was getting nowhere with his own talk. Not one of the three men who held the power of the Bavarian state in their hands had agreed to join him, even at pistol point. The putsch wasn't going according to plan. Then Hitler acted on a sudden impulse. Without a further word, he dashed back into the hall, mounted the tribune, faced the sullen crowd and announced that the members of the triumvirate in the next room had joined him in forming a new national government.

"The Bavarian Ministry," he shouted, "is removed. . . . The government of the November criminals and the Reich President are declared to be removed. A new national government will be named this very day here in Munich. A German National Army will be formed immediately. . . . I propose that, until accounts have been finally settled with the November criminals, the direction of policy in the National Government be taken over by me. Ludendorff will take over the leadership of the German National Army. . . . The task of the provisional German National Government is to organize the march on that sinful Babel, Berlin, and save the German people. . . . Tomorrow will find either a National Government in Germany or us dead!"

Not for the first time and certainly not for the last, Hitler had told a masterful lie, and it worked. When the gathering heard that Kahr, General von Lossow and Police Chief von Seisser had joined Hitler its mood abruptly changed. There were loud cheers, and the sound of them impressed the three men still locked up in the little side room.

Scheubner-Richter now produced General Ludendorff, as if out of a hat. The war hero was furious with Hitler for pulling such a complete surprise on him, and when, once closeted in the side room, he learned that the former corporal and not he was to be the dictator of Germany his resentment was compounded. He spoke scarcely a word to the brash young man. But Hitler did not mind so long as Ludendorff lent his famous name to the desperate undertaking and won over the three recalcitrant Bavarian leaders who thus far had failed to respond to his own exhortations and threats. This Ludendorff proceeded to do. It was now a question of a great national cause, he said, and he advised the gentlemen to co-operate. Awed by the attention of the generalissimo, the trio appeared to give in, though later Lossow denied that he had agreed to place himself under Ludendorff's command. For a few minutes Kahr fussed over the question of restoring the Wittelsbach monarchy, which was so dear to him. Finally he said he would co-operate as the "King's deputy."

Ludendorff's timely arrival had saved Hitler. Overjoyed at this lucky break, he led the others back to the platform, where each made a brief speech and swore loyalty to each other and to the new regime. The crowd leaped on chairs and tables in a delirium of enthusiasm. Hitler beamed with joy. "He had a childlike, frank expression of happiness that I shall never forget," an eminent historian [Karl Alexander von Mueller] who was present later declared. . . .

Hitler Meets Resistance from the Bavarian Government

Then news came of a clash between storm troopers of one of the fighting leagues, the Bund Oberland, and regular troops at the Army Engineers' barracks. Hitler decided to drive to the scene and settle the matter personally, leaving the beer hall in charge of Ludendorff.

This turned out to be a fatal error. Lossow was the first to slip away. He informed Ludendorff he must hurry to his office at Army headquarters to give the necessary orders. When Scheubner-Richter objected, Ludendorff rejoined stiffly, "I forbid you to doubt the word of a German officer." Kahr and Seisser vanished too.

Hitler, in high spirits, returned to the Buergerbräu to find that the birds had flown the coop. This was the first blow of the evening and it stunned him. He had confidently expected to find his "ministers" busy at their new tasks while Ludendorff and Lossow worked out plans for the march on Berlin. But almost nothing was being done. Not even Munich was being occupied by the revolutionary forces. Roehm, at the head of a detachment of storm troopers from another fighting league, the Reichskriegsflagge, had seized Army headquarters at the War Ministry in the Schoenfeldstrasse but no other strategic centers were occupied, not even the telegraph office, over whose wires news of the coup went out to Berlin and orders came back, from General von Seeckt to the Army in Bavaria, to suppress the putsch. . . .

Hitler and Ludendorff joined Roehm at the ministry for a time, to take stock of the situation. Roehm was shocked to find that no one besides himself had taken military action and occupied the key centers. Hitler tried desperately to re-establish contact with Lossow, Kahr and Seisser. Messengers were dispatched to the 19th Infantry barracks in the name of Ludendorff but they did not return. Poehner, the former Munich police chief and now one of Hitler's supporters, was sent with Major Huehnlein and a band of the S.A. troopers to occupy police headquarters. They were promptly arrested there. . . .

The triumph which earlier in the evening had seemed to Hitler so near and so easily won was rapidly fading with the night. The basis for a successful political revolution on which he had always insisted—the support of existing institutions such as the Army, the police, the political group in power—was now crumbling. Not even Ludendorff's magic name, it was now clear, had won over the armed forces of the state. Hitler suggested that perhaps the situation could be retrieved if he and the General withdrew to the countryside near Rosenheim and rallied the peasants behind the armed bands for an assault on Munich, but Ludendorff promptly rejected the idea. . . .

Hitler had planned a putsch, not a civil war. Despite his feverish state of excitement he was in sufficient control of himself to realize that he lacked the strength to overcome the police and the Army. He had wanted to make a revolution *with* the armed forces, not *against* them. Blood-thirsty though he had been in his recent speeches and during the hours he held the Bavarian triumvirs at gunpoint, he shrank from the idea of men united in their hatred of the Republic shedding the blood of each other. . . .

The Putsch Takes to the Streets

To the wavering young Nazi leader Ludendorff now proposed a plan of his own that might still bring them victory and yet avoid bloodshed. German soldiers, even German police—who were mostly ex-soldiers—would never dare, he was sure, to fire on the legendary commander who had led them to great victories on both the Eastern and the Western fronts. He and Hitler would march with their followers to the center of the city and take it over. Not only would the police and the Army not dare to oppose him, he was certain; they would join him and fight under his orders. Though somewhat skeptical, Hitler agreed. There seemed no other way out. . . .

Toward eleven o'clock on the morning of November 9, the anniversary of the proclamation of the German Republic, Hitler and Ludendorff led a column of some three thousand storm troopers out of the gardens of the Buergerbräukeller and headed for the center of Munich. Beside them in the front rank marched Goering, commander of the S.A., Scheubner-Richter, Rosenberg, Ulrich Graf, Hitler's bodyguard, and half a dozen other Nazi officials and leaders of the Kampfbund. A swastika flag and a banner of the Bund Oberland were unfurled at the head of the column. Not far behind the first ranks a truck chugged along, loaded with machine guns and machine gunners. The storm troopers carried carbines, slung over their shoulders, some with fixed bayonets. Hitler brandished his revolver. Not a very formidable armed force, but Ludendorff, who had commanded millions of Germany's finest troops, apparently thought it sufficient for his purposes.

A few hundred yards north of the beer cellar the rebels met their first obstacle. On the Ludwig Bridge, which leads over the River Isar toward the center of the city, stood a detachment of armed police barring the route. Goering sprang forward and, addressing the police commander, threatened to shoot a number of hostages he said he had in the rear of his column if the police fired on his men. During the night Hess and others had rounded up a number of hostages, including two cabinet members, for just such a contingency. Whether Goering was bluffing or not, the police commander apparently believed he was not and let the column file over the bridge unmolested. . . .

Shortly after noon the marchers neared their objective, the War Ministry, where Roehm and his storm troopers were surrounded by soldiers of the Reichswehr. Neither besiegers nor besieged had yet fired a shot. Roehm and his men were all ex-soldiers and they had many wartime comrades on the other side of the barbed wire. Neither side had any heart for killing. . . .

But once again the Nazis tried to talk their way through. One of them, the faithful bodyguard Ulrich Graf, stepped forward and cried out to the police officer in charge, "Don't shoot! His Excellency Ludendorff is coming!" Even at this crucial, perilous moment, a German revolutionary, even an old amateur wrestler and professional bouncer, remembered to give a gentleman his proper title. Hitler added another cry. "Surrender! Surrender!" he called out. But the unknown police officer did not surrender. Apparently Ludendorff's name had no magic sound for him; this was the police, not the Army. . . .

At any rate a shot was fired and in the next instant a volley of shots rang out from both sides, spelling in that instant the doom of Hitler's hopes. Scheubner-Richter fell, mortally wounded. Goering went down with a serious wound in his thigh. Within sixty seconds the firing stopped, but the street was already littered with fallen bodies—sixteen Nazis and three police dead or dying, many more wounded and the rest, including Hitler, clutching the pavement to save their lives. . . .

Hitler Abandons the Putsch

The future Chancellor of the Third Reich was the first to scamper to safety. He had locked his left arm with the right arm of Scheubner-Richter (a curious but perhaps revealing gesture) as the column approached the police cordon, and when the latter fell he pulled Hitler down to the pavement with him. Perhaps Hitler thought he had been wounded; he suffered sharp pains which, it was found later, came from a dislocated shoulder. But the fact remains that according to the testimony of one of his own Nazi followers in the column, the physician Dr. Walther Schulz, which was supported by several other witnesses, Hitler "was the first to get up and turn back," leaving his dead and wounded comrades lying in the street. He was hustled into a waiting motorcar and spirited off to the country home of [Ernst Franz Hanfstaengl, Hitler's companion called Putzi] at Uffing, where Putzi's wife and sister nursed him and where, two days later, he was arrested. . . .

Within a few days all the rebel leaders except Goering and Hess were rounded up and jailed. The Nazi putsch had ended in a fiasco. The party was dissolved. National Socialism, to all appearances, was dead. Its dictatorial leader, who had run away at the first hail of bullets, seemed utterly discredited, his meteoric political career at an end.

Trial for Treason

As things turned out, that career was merely interrupted, and not for long. Hitler was shrewd enough to see that his trial, far from finishing him, would provide a new platform from which he could not only discredit the compromised authorities who had arrested him but—and this was more important—for the first time make his name known far beyond the confines of Bavaria and indeed of Germany itself. He was well aware that correspondents of the world press as well as of the leading German newspapers were flocking to Munich to cover the trial, which began on February 26, 1924, before a special court sitting in the old Infantry School in the Blutenburgstrasse. By the time it had ended twenty-four days later Hitler had transformed defeat into triumph, made Kahr, Lossow and Seisser share his guilt in the public mind to their ruin, impressed the German people with his eloquence and the fervor of his nationalism, and emblazoned his name on the front pages of the world. . . .

Ludendorff was acquitted. Hitler and the other accused were found guilty. But in the face of the law—Article 81 of the German Penal Code—which declared that "whosoever—attempts to alter by force the Constitution of the German Reich or of any German state shall be punished by lifelong imprisonment," Hitler was sentenced to five years' imprisonment in the old fortress of Landsberg. Even then the lay judges protested the severity of the sentence, but they were assured by the presiding judge that the prisoner would be eligible for parole after he had served six months. Efforts of the police to get Hitler deported as a foreigner—he still held Austrian citizenship—came to nothing. The sentences were imposed on April 1, 1924. A little less than nine months later, on December 20, Hitler was released from prison, free to resume his fight to overthrow the democratic state. . . .

The putsch, even though it was a fiasco, made Hitler a national figure and, in the eyes of many, a patriot and a hero. Nazi propaganda soon transformed it into one of the great legends of the movement. . . .

That summer of 1924 in the old fortress at Landsberg, high above the River Lech, Adolf Hitler, who was treated as an honored guest, with a room of his own and a splendid view, cleared out the visitors who flocked to pay him homage and bring him gifts, summoned the faithful Rudolf Hess, who had finally returned to Munich and received a sentence, and began to dictate to him chapter after chapter of a book [*Mein Kampf*].

Hitler's Mission to Exterminate the Jews

Lucy S. Dawidowicz

In the following selection Lucy S. Dawidowicz writes that at the center of all of Hitler's actions up to and throughout World War II was his goal to annihilate the Jewish people. By 1936 Jewish discrimination was well under way in Germany, and Hitler was free to expand his "mission" beyond Germany's borders by invading foreign nations. Dawidowicz concludes that Hitler was able to bring his plans to fruition due to a combination of circumstances, including his charismatic leadership, a German tradition of anti-Semitism, and the humiliation and hardship that had befallen the German people in the wake of World War I.

Dawidowicz is a graduate of Columbia University. She studied East European Jewish life at the Yivo Institute for Jewish Research, formerly in Poland. She is also the author of *The Golden Tradition: Jewish Life and Thought in Eastern Europe* and *The Holocaust Reader*.

❧ ❧ ❧

Once Hitler adopted an ideological position, even a strategic one, he adhered to it with limpetlike fixity, fearful lest he be accused, if he changed his mind, of incertitude or capriciousness on "essential questions." He had long-range plans to realize his ideological goals, and the destruction of the Jews was at their center.

The grand design was in his head. He did not spell it out in concrete strategy. Nothing was written down. (On April 29, 1937, he advised NSDAP [Nazi Party] leaders: "Everything that can be discussed should *never* be put in writing, never!") He even elevated his tactics of secrecy into a strategic principle: as few people as possible to know as little as possible as late as possible.

The implementation of his plans was contingent on the opportunism of the moment or the expediency of delay. As head of both the German state and the National Socialist movement, he had to weigh the urgent passions of the little man in the party against the foreign-policy interests of the state, and to balance his own desire for surprise attack with the state's readiness to mount one. Often he decided suddenly that the opportune occasion had arrived to carry out a specific aspect of his program, and then the practical work had quickly to be improvised.

The First Phase

In Hitler's schema, the removal of the Jews from posts in the state apparatus and from society's cultural and educational institutions represented, along with the remilitarization of Germany, the first phase of his program, the internal cleansing and healing of Germany. Whereas the anti-Jewish legislation of 1933 was for him merely the prerequisite for later stages of his program that would culminate in the Final Solution, this undoing of the emancipation of the German Jews represented for the conventional anti-Semites the attainment of their political ambitions. That was the time when the widest consensus existed in Germany with regard to anti-Semitism, when the values and goals of the conventional anti-Semites were identical and undistinguishable from those of the radical anti-Semites. That particular convergence made it easier for the conventional anti-Semites subsequently to acquiesce to the radical anti-Semitic program.

At the National Socialist party congress in Nuremberg in September 1935, Hitler introduced new anti-Jewish legislation, describing these laws as a repayment of a debt of gratitude to the National Socialist party, under whose aegis Germany had regained her freedom, and as the fulfillment of an important plank of the movement's program. The Reich Citizenship Law, depriving the German Jews of the rights and protections of citizenship, marked the goal of conventional anti-Semitism—the total disenfranchisement of the Jews.

The Law for the Protection of German Blood and German Honor, on the other hand, even though it drew heavily upon a half-century's tradition of racist anti-Semitism, was a new departure. With its implementing decrees and with those of the Reich Citizenship Law, it initiated Hitler's program of radical anti-Semitism, with the process of identifying and isolating the Jews from the non-Jews, readying them, as it were, for their later fate.

The Nuremberg Laws were a watershed also in another respect, to which Hitler alluded ominously. In introducing the Law for the Protection of German Blood and German Honor, he said that it was "an attempt to regulate by law a problem which, in the event of repeated failure, would have to be transferred by law to the National Socialist party for final solution." He was, it now appears, indicating that the state had come to the end of its competency in handling the Jewish question and that thenceforth all anti-Jewish measures would be carried out by the party. In this period, too, he spoke of sweeping plans for the Jews, involving ghettos and possibly a reservation, and on another occasion he talked of carrying out the "euthanasia" murder program once war came.

The Second Phase

By the summer of 1936, Hitler believed that the first phase of his program—the internal domestic stage—was virtually completed and in August, having composed a memorandum on the Four Year Plan, [a plan for economic recovery], he entered into preparations for the second phase—aggression and war. That memorandum, with its ideological justification for a war against "Jewish Bolshevism," transformed *Mein Kampf* into state policy. The doctrine of the party leader now became the plan for the state. The annihilation of the Jews, who are explicitly referred to as the power behind Bolshevism, is implicit in Hitler's familiar rhetorical construction (italicized in the original): *"For a victory of Bolshevism over Germany would not lead to a Versailles Treaty but to the final destruction, indeed to the annihilation, of the German people."* As further clarification, Hitler specified that the Reichstag would have to pass a law expropriating the Jews. Thus the expropriation of the Jews had become, in Hitler's thinking, correlated with the advancement of his war plans. That decision explains why Hitler rejected the insistent demands of the National Socialist movement between 1935 and 1938 to plunder Jewish property and posessions. . . .

Reverting to Medievalism

If the plans for dealing with the Jews were vague and nonspecific, so were the plans for military invasion, as the Hossbach protocol[1] reveals. Hitler's military and diplomatic staffs were appalled to learn in November 1937 of Hitler's intentions to invade Austria and Czechoslovakia in 1938, not so much because of the suddenness with which they had to confront these plans, but because of lack of preparation. Their demurral, however, cost them their posts and careers, for Hitler remained inflexible, committed to his timetable. The Austrian invasion advanced smoothly, but [English prime minister Neville] Chamberlain's intervention in Czechoslovakia frustrated Hitler's plans. It appears that he had intended, under cover of the seizure of Czechoslovakia, to carry out the expropriation of the Jews, for the first National Socialist legislation in this area was issued early in 1938. Hitler no doubt counted on the general public upheaval over Czechoslovakia to muffle protests about robbing the Jews.

Thwarted by Chamberlain, but impatient to move ahead according to his schedule, Hitler took the first opportunity that would give him apparent justification to expropriate the Jews: the assassination of [Ernest] vom Rath. That opportunism proved doubly useful, for it gave the little Nazi a last chance for a fling. The pogrom and the expropriation were not really part of Hitler's new, radical anti-Semitism, but rather a reversion to medievalism, when Jews were subjected not only to violence, but to all sorts of taxes, fines, levies, exactions, amercements, and confiscations. In the Middle Ages complete expropriation went hand in hand with expulsion, and for the brief period that National Socialist pressure for Jewish emigration intensified following the Kristallnach,[2] Hitler seemed to be emulating [French kings] Edward I and Philip the Fair. But

1. a memorandum written by Hitler's army adjunct Colonel Count Friedrich Hossbach after a November 1937 meeting of Hitler and high-ranking Nazis   2. Night of Broken Glass, a Jewish pogrom that began on November 9, 1938

pressure for emigration was, in Hitler's plans, only by-play. After the Kristallnacht the Jews in Germany became little more than hostages, perhaps no different from the way Hitler and [Hermann] Esser had envisaged the situation in 1923. The Reichszentrale, which [Hermann] Göring had instructed [SS chief Heinrich Himmler's number-two man, Reinhard] Heydrich to set up on January 24, 1939, effectively put the Jews at the mercy of the police and SD [Sicherheitsdienst, the security branch of the SS]. (Probably then, Heydrich was made a party to the plan to destroy the Jews.)

An Irreversible Mission

On January 30, 1939, Hitler made his declaration of war against the Jews, promising "the destruction of the Jewish race in Europe." The decision to proceed with this irreversible mission had already been taken. Thenceforth the Final Solution entered the stage of practical planning for implementation. Hitler's first opportunity to put into practice his ideas about killing the crippled and insane presented itself at this time, and shortly thereafter, on April 3, 1939, he instructed [the Chief of the high command of the armed forces, Wilhelm] Keitel to start planning the invasion of Poland.

Hitler's gamble, then, was on a quick military victory in Poland, to be completed before Russia could gather wits or forces to act. Afterward he would consolidate his position, using Poland as the launching pad for his invasion of Russia. (The rapprochement with Russia, ideologically embarrassing but tactically expedient, did not at all affect his long-range plans, but merely eased his short-range military risks.) While planning the Polish invasion, Hitler, Himmler, and Heydrich worked out the first stage of the Final Solution, concentrating the Jews while consolidating the Polish gains. Heydrich's instructions to the chiefs of the Einsatzgruppen [mobile killing units] on September 21, 1939, are clear enough about present program and future intentions. The second, ultimate stage of the Final Solution was to be synchronized with the attack on Russia, when "Jewish Bolshevism" would be destroyed. . . .

A Two-Pronged Attack

In December 1940 Operation Barbarossa [the Russian invasion] entered the formal planning stage, and Hitler then no doubt explored with Himmler, and perhaps Heydrich, various practical possibilities for the last stage of the Final Solution. By February 1941 they had decided on a two-pronged attack against the Jews. In the active war zone, the Einsatzgruppen would coordinate their murder attack on the Jews with the military invasion. The rest of the European Jews in countries under German occupation or governed by rulers sympathetic to Germany would be brought to annihilation camps in or near the Generalgouvernement of Poland. . . . All the decisions had been taken. The rest was a matter of technology, administrative clearance, and efficient operation. Through a maze of time Hitler's decision of November 1918 led to Operation Barbarossa. There never had been any ideological deviation or wavering determination. In the end only the question of opportunity mattered.

A Radical Doctrine of Mass Murder

The Final Solution grew out of a matrix formed by traditional anti-Semitism, the paranoid delusions that seized Germany after World War I, and the emergence of Hitler and the National Socialist movement. Without Hitler, the charismatic political leader, who believed he had a mission to annihilate the Jews, the Final Solution would not have occurred. Without that assertive and enduring tradition of anti-Semitism by which the

Germans sought self-definition, Hitler would not have had the fecund soil in which to grow his organization and spread its propaganda. Without the paranoid delusion of the Dolchstoss[3] that masses of Germans shared in the wake of Germany's military defeat, political upheavals, economic distress, and humiliations of the Versailles Treaty, Hitler could not have transformed the German brand of conventional anti-Semitism into a radical doctrine of mass murder.

Anti-Semitism was the core of Hitler's system of beliefs and the central motivation for his policies. He believed himself to be the savior who would bring redemption to the German people through the annihilation of the Jews, that people who embodied, in his eyes, the Satanic hosts. When he spoke or wrote about his "holy mission," he used words associated with chiliastic prophecy (not only in the millennial concept literally rendered as the "Thousand Year Reich"), like "consecration," "salvation," "redemption," "resurrection," "God's will." The murder of the Jews, in his fantasies, was commanded by divine providence, and he was the chosen instrument for that task. He referred often to his "mission," but nowhere so explicitly as in *Mein Kampf:* "Hence today I believe that I am acting in accordance with the will of the Almighty Creator: *by defending myself against the Jew, I am fighting for the work of the Lord.*" From the moment he made his entrance on the historical stage until his death in a Berlin bunker, this sense of messianic mission never departed from him, nor could any appeal to reason deflect him from pursuing his murderous purpose.

---

3. *Dolchstoss* means "stab in the back" in German. This term refers to the belief that Germany had not been defeated in World War I, but that Germans had been betrayed by Jews and Socialists.

Profiles · in · History

The Elite of the
Third Reich

Paul Joseph Goebbels: The Little Mouse General

Louis P. Lochner

Because he was a small, slight man who walked with a limp, Paul Joseph Goebbels felt inferior and inadequate from an early age, but in Adolf Hitler and the Nazi Party, Goebbels found the personal and professional validation he was seeking. Despite his high-ranking Nazi position of minister of propaganda and public enlightenment, however, Goebbels was never taken seriously by other members of the Nazi elite, who ridiculed his small stature and called him "the Little Mouse General." An avid diarist, Goebbels faithfully recorded the evolution of the Nazi Party and the Führer's activities because he believed his journals would be the only accurate record of the development and activities of the Third Reich. Some of the diary pages upon which this selection is based were found after World War II, singed and smoke-scented among the ruins of the Reich chancellery.

Louis P. Lochner was a journalist with the Associated Press in Berlin who personally interviewed Goebbels and other high-ranking Nazis, including Hitler, edited and

Louis P. Lochner, *The Goebbels Diaries: 1942–1943*. New York: Doubleday, 1948. Copyright © 1948 by Fireside Press, Inc. Reproduced by permission.

translated Goebbels's diaries from the years 1942 through 1943. In 1939 Lochner received the Pulitzer Prize for distinguished service as a foreign correspondent for his reporting of the events of World War II. In the following excerpt from his introduction to the diaries, Lochner portrays Goebbels as a fastidious workaholic who was one of the Führer's closest friends and comrades. Lochner offers a retrospective look at the ambition and lust for power that directed Goebbels to aid and abet Hitler's reign of terror.

❦   ❦   ❦

(P.aul) Joseph Goebbels was born October 29, 1897, in the smoky factory town of Rheydt in the Rhineland. He was the son of a factory foreman, Fritz Goebbels, and his wife, Maria Odenhausen, a blacksmith's daughter. His parents were devout Roman Catholics, as were his various relations.

The boy Joseph—or, as he was nicknamed, Jupp (pronounced Youp)—attended one of the Catholic grade schools of this textile center of 30,000 inhabitants, and also went through the Gymnasium, or high school, of his native city. He was rejected for military service during World War I because of a deformed foot.

He managed to secure a number of Catholic scholarships and attended eight famous German universities—Bonn, Freiburg, Wuerzburg, Munich, Cologne, Frankfurt, Berlin, and finally Heidelberg, where he took his Ph.D. degree in 1921 at the age of twenty-four. He studied history, philology, and the history of art and literature.

Years of Chaos

His ambition was to be a writer. The year of his graduation at Heidelberg he wrote an unsuccessful novel, *Michael*, and followed it by two plays, *Blood Seed* (*Blut-*

saat) and *The Wanderer* (*Der Wanderer*), which no producer would accept. He also applied, unsuccessfully, for a reporter's job on the *Berliner Tageblatt*, internationally famed liberal daily.

All these experiences, together with the loss of the war and the collapse of the German Empire, embittered him and kept him restlessly wandering from Rheydt to Cologne, Berlin, and Munich, until, rather by accident, he heard Adolf Hitler speak at Munich in 1922.

Young Joseph Goebbels first tried to interest university students in Hitler's message and thereby discovered that he had the gift of eloquence. That was just the sort of man Hitler needed. The Fuehrer tested his disciple's abilities in the Rhine and Ruhr, then under Allied occupation. Working under an assumed name, Goebbels managed to win converts to Nazism and located his office at Hattingen in the Ruhr Valley. In 1924 the French occupation authorities ejected him.

Goebbels then drifted to Elberfeld, where he became editor of a Nazi organ, *Voelkische Freiheit* (Racist Freedom). His articles against the French Negro troops of occupation were especially vitriolic. That same year he was appointed business manager for the Nazi gau, or district, of Rhine-Ruhr.

I have been fortunate in having access to an important document dealing with this period of Goebbels's life. Former President [Herbert] Hoover, during a visit to Germany in 1946, was given a hand-written diary kept by Dr. Goebbels from August 12, 1925, to October 16, 1926, which he has kindly placed at my disposal. This diary is important in its revelation of a little scoundrel in training to become a great scoundrel. In addition, it gives valuable evidence of the authenticity of the later diaries.

The accounts of those days are replete with references to beer-hall fights, street brawls, and encounters with the police. Goebbels turned his back completely upon the church in which he was raised, and abandoned the faith of his fathers.

Father and Mother Goebbels were greatly displeased at their son's apostasy. He complains, on the occasion of a visit to his parents at Rheydt, September 11, 1925: "Father is serious and uncommunicative. That depresses me." He writes on the occasion of his twenty-eighth birthday at Elberfeld: "Not a word from home. How hurt I feel!" Two days later he observes: "Not a word from home for my birthday, nor anything else. That rather pains me. I am gradually losing contact.". . .

Hitler's Glorification

If one had only the typewritten diaries to go by, one might conclude from the adulation amounting almost to deification of the Fuehrer that Goebbels was writing with a view to expediency rather than from conviction—witness an entry like that of March 19, 1942: "As long as he [the Fuehrer] lives and is among us in good health, as long as he can give us the strength of his spirit and the power of his manliness, no evil can touch us." Could such an apotheosis have been written in sincerity by as coldly calculating a realist as Joseph Goebbels, by a man who from time to time even disagreed with the leader?

Here again the earlier diaries furnish corroborative evidence. They prove that Joseph Goebbels, who otherwise seemed to love no one but himself and his children, did indeed adore Adolf Hitler. . . .

November 6, 1995: "Brunswick. . . .

Wit, irony, humor, sarcasm, earnestness, passion, white heat—all this is contained in his speech. This man has everything it takes to be king. The great tribune of the people. The coming dictator."

November 23, 1925: "Plauen. I arrive. Hitler is there. My joy is great. He greets me like an old friend.

And lavishes attention on me. I have him all to myself. What a guy (*So ein Kerl!*). . . ."

When one reads these earlier diary entries, one cannot but conclude that the diaries of 1942 and 1943 are sincere in their portrayal of a very close relationship of mutual trust between Hitler and Goebbels. The sequel to the diaries, too, bears testimony to the sincerity of Goebbels's adoration of his Fuehrer and to the sincerity of the diaries: he committed suicide immediately after Hitler passed out of his life!

The Diaries Reveal Goebbels's Attitudes

Unfortunately space does not permit the systematic inclusion of excerpts from the earlier handwriting diaries. Nevertheless, some sections of them seem to me essential for a proper understanding of Goebbels and his time.

There is, first of all, Goebbels's revelation of his attitude toward his fellow men. The diaries for 1942–43 convey this only by inference. On August 12, 1925, however, he put down in black and white: "As soon as I am with a person for three days, I don't like him any longer; and if I am with him for a whole week, I hate him like the plague."

On October 15, 1925, he observed, "I have learned to despise the human being from the bottom of my soul. He makes me sick in my stomach. Phooey!"

On April 24, 1926, he had occasion to write: "Much dirt and many intrigues. The human being is a *canaille*."

On August 9, 1926, he found that "The only real friend one has in the end is the dog." This was followed on August 17 with a further tribute to his dog Benno: "The more I get to know the human species, the more I care for my Benno.". . .

The earlier diaries afford insight into the little doctor's personal habits for which one looks in vain in the 1942–43 versions: his love life. Goebbels's amours were a matter of notoriety throughout Germany. His philandering even after he had become a Reich Minister was so well known and so scandalous that his wife, Magda, would on more than one occasion have sued for divorce had not Hitler insisted that he would stand for no marital scandal in the case of a person so highly placed as Dr. Goebbels. . . .

A Radical Disciple

Two entries (among others) in the earlier diaries show how close the then young agitator felt to the Communists:

October 23, 1925: "In the final analysis it would be better for us to end our existence under Bolshevism than to endure slavery under capitalism."

January 31, 1926: "I think it is terrible that we and the Communists are bashing in each other's heads. . . . Where can we get together sometime with the leading Communists?"

It was over the issue of radicalism, in fact, that Goebbels in 1926 for a while entertained grave doubts about Adolf Hitler.

On February 15, 1926, Goebbels heard the Fuehrer speak at Bamberg. The little doctor wrote:

"Hitler talked for two hours. I feel as though someone had beaten me. What sort of a Hitler is this? A reactionary? Extremely lacking in poise and assuredness. Russian question: quite off the beam. Italy and England our natural allies! Terrible! Our task, he says, is the destruction of Bolshevism. Bolshevism is a Jewish creation. We must break Russia. Two hundred and eighty millons! . . .

"I am unable to say a word. I feel as though someone had hit me over the head. . . . How my heart hurts! . . . I should like to cry. . . .

"Certainly one of the greatest disappointments of my

life. I no longer have complete faith in Hitler. That is the terrible thing about it: my props have been taken from under me. I am only half a person."

A month later, however, Goebbels begins to regain confidence that Hitler, after all, is right. On March 13 he wrote:

"I read Adolf Hitler's *The South Tyrol Question and the Problem of Germany's Alliances*, a wonderfully clear and broad-minded brochure. He's a great guy, all right— our chief."

His last doubts were dispelled when he heard Hitler speak in Munich on April 13. Here is the story of his capitulation:

"Hitler arrived. . . . He spoke for three hours. Brilliantly. He can make you doubt your own views. Italy and England our allies. Russia wants to devour us. All that is contained in his brochure and in the second volume of *Mein Kempf* which is to appear soon.

"We disagree. We ask questions. He gives brilliant replies. I love him. The social question: he opens great new vistas. He has thought everything through. His ideal: a just collectivism and individualism. As to soil— everything on and under it belongs to the people. Production to be creative and individualistic. Trusts, transportation, et cetera, to be socialized. That's something! He has thought it all through. I am now at ease about him. He is a he-man. He takes everything into account. A hothead like that can be my leader. I bow to the greater man, to the political genius.". . .

From the beginning of his career as a National Socialist Goebbels was a glutton for work. He spoke night after night, edited his paper, attended to a multitude of details of political organization, and still found time with Gregor Strasser [an earlier Hitler supporter who broke away from Nazism] to start the *National-Sozialistische Briefe* (National Socialist Letters) which were soon eagerly read by German workers. Goebbels could truly claim that he and Strasser secured Hitler his working-class following—Hitler himself had appealed mainly to the middle class, the petty bourgeoisie, as well as to ardent nationalists of every persuasion. . . .

Goebbels Rises in Power

The Goebbels-Strasser duumvirate did not last long. At the Nazi party convention of 1926 at Bamberg, Bavaria, Goebbels soon sensed that Strasser and the Fuehrer did not see eye to eye, and decided his bread was buttered on the Hitler side. He sided with his idol against his friend. Hitler rewarded him on November 9, the anniversary of the ill-fated beer-cellar putsch of 1923, by making him Gauleiter for Greater Berlin, a task well calculated to test to the full the abilities of the little doctor, as an organizer, writer, strategist, and political leader.

The capital in those days was known as *das rote Berlin* (Red Berlin). It polled a large Communist vote, and the Socialists were the dominating party. That was grist for the fiery doctor's mill. Street brawls and beer-hall fights were the order of the day. In 1927 Goebbels founded a weekly paper, *Der Angriff* (The Attack), which by 1929 became a biweekly and from 1930 on a daily. If the Communists hitherto held a monopoly on guttersnipe vituperative language, they now had a thing or two to learn from the venomous Nazi editor.

Goebbels's career as a parliamentarian began in 1928, when he was elected to the German Reichstag. A year later he also became a town councillor of Berlin. . . .

Adolf Hitler was much impressed with *der gescheite Dr. Goebbels* (the cleverly intelligent Dr. Goebbels). . . . This young man showed that he possessed something which many an older politician could well envy him: an uncanny understanding of the psychology of the German people. Goebbels was very often way off in his estimate of foreign nations; however, he did know his fellow Germans.

In 1929 Hitler made the then thirty-two-year-old Goebbels Reich Propaganda Leader of the Nazi party. "Propaganda has only one object," the new Reichsleiter said on one occasion—"to conquer the masses. Every means that furthers this aim is good; every means that hinders it is bad." He had already given samples of his skill at propaganda not only by his articles and the innumerable handbills and posters he designed, but also in the books, all written before 1930, *The Unknown SA Man, Lenin or Hitler? The Second Revolution, Buch Isidor,* and *Knorke.*

Goebbels was quite willing to admit that his speeches and writings were usually on the "primitive" side. "Our propaganda is primitive," The Associated Press reported him as saying, "because the people think primitively. We speak the language the people understand.". . .

Reich Minister

January 30, 1933, brought the accession of Adolf Hitler to undreamed-of power. In the first official announcements the name of Dr. Goebbels was conspicuously absent. Hermann Goering and Wilhelm Frick were the only two National Socialists besides Adolf Hitler in the first Hitler cabinet.

Goebbels could well afford to wait. Hitler had great plans for him. On June 30, 1933, he decreed the establishment of a new cabinet office, that of Reich Ministry for Public Enlightenment and Propaganda, with Joseph Goebbels as its head, stating that the new venture would be "responsible for all tasks having to do with influencing the mental and spiritual life of the nation, for winning allegiance to the state, its culture and economy, for informing the public at home and abroad about the nation, and for administering all institutions and installations contributing to these ends."

Decree followed decree, expanding his powers and functions. There was the Reich Culture Chamber Law of September 22, 1933, channeling all intellectual and cultural life into this one chamber with its six sub-chambers (Reich Radio Chamber, Reich Theater Chamber, Reich Press Chamber, et cetera) and appointing Goebbels as president which, under Nazism, meant dictator. There was the Journalists' Law of October 4, 1933, which made all newsmen servants of the state and subject to license by Goebbels. There was the decree of November 26, 1936, forbidding all artistic criticism.

Soon Goebbels unblushingly forbade the publication of speeches by cabinet members. He even decreed that nobody could quote past utterances of the Fuehrer without the approval of his Propaganda Ministry.

Goebbels unscrupulously used his vast powers to foster anti-Semitism by fabricating stories about atrocities allegedly committed by the Jews. As World War II loomed on the horizon—and no Nazi besides Hitler himself knew better than Goebbels how certain it was to come—he kept up a constant barrage of stories alleging maltreatment and even torture of German nationals by the populations of neighboring states.

He thus prepared the ground well for Hitler's war on civilization.

Dictator in Domestic Affairs

Even after his phenomenal rise to power Goebbels never lost sight of the desirability of making himself *persona gratissima* [an important person] to Adolf Hitler. He could not impress Hitler with a war record like that of Hermann Goering, the *Pour le Mérite* aviation ace of World War I, as he was physically incapacitated for military service. The Fuehrer, however, laid great stress upon large families.

Goebbels had married the comely and socially presentable Magda, a woman who in her first marriage to a German industrialist named Quandt already had one son, Harald. It was a matter of common gossip in Berlin society circles that Joseph Goebbels insisted that his wife deliver one baby a year. His offspring consisted of six children at the end of the Hitler regime. Goebbels, coldly calculating that these children would probably not have much of a chance in a world to which Nazism was anathema, poisoned them all and prevailed upon Magda likewise to take poison [after Hitler's death].

Before the war, however, the wife and children were quite an asset in Goebbels's bid for Hitler's affection. The children were taught to say nice things to "Onkel Adolf." Goebbels records with pride that the Fuehrer during his private talks usually inquired about Hilde, Holde, and Helga. He apparently knew the three younger children, Heide, Hedda, and Helmuth less well. Also, he vowed that after the war he would see to it that his family devote itself to his idol even more than before the great conflict.

Such was the Joseph Goebbels of pre–World War II days, such were his powers. The diaries will show that even these powers did not satiate his inordinate ambition, but that he used the Fuehrer's absence at the military front virtually to set himself up as dictator in domestic affairs. . . .

This diminutive man, one of the most versatile spellbinders Germany has had in generations, was absolutely cool and self-possessed while at the same time he gave the impression of being deeply stirred and carried away by his own eloquence.

His voice, of a deeply resonant quality, seemed to quiver with emotion. His gestures seemed passionate. His general attitude seemed to be that of a man so wrapped up in his fanaticism that time meant nothing so long as he had a message to deliver.

I noticed something else, however: his fascinatingly delicate hands moved in powerful gestures without the slightest trembling and belied the quiver in his voice. His gestures, although seemingly spontaneous, indicated careful planning, for he always threw himself into position for a particular gesture before actually beginning to execute it. Beside him lay a watch which he consulted from time to time by a stealthy glance, clearly showing that he was well aware of the passage of time.

In short, here was a showman who knew exactly what he was doing every moment and who calculated in advance the effect of every spoken word and every gesture. Disgustingly grating though the raucous voice of Adolf Hitler was and disturbing though the frequent breaks in his voice were as he talked himself into a high pitch of frenzied exaltation, the hearer nevertheless had the impression that here was a man who believed what he said or at least intoxicated himself into this belief on hearing his own fulminations. With Goebbels I had the feeling that he would have defended Communism, monarchy, or even democracy with the same pathos and emotion, yes, even the same fanaticism, had his idol, Hitler, chosen to sponsor any of these. . . .

Denying Kristallnacht

A striking example of Goebbels's capacity for unabashed prevarication was given the foreign correspondents accredited at Berlin on November 10, 1938, the day after Hitler had given the "go" sign to his hordes to loot Jewish shops, demolish Jewish property, set fire to synagogues, and arrest innocent Jews. We were asked to come to the Propaganda Ministry late that forenoon, as Dr. Goebbels wished to make a statement. . . .

Suddenly he entered with quick, nervous steps, invited us to stand in a semicircle about him, and then delivered a declaration to the effect that "all the accounts that have come to your ears about alleged looting and destruction of Jewish property are a stinking lie (*sind erstunken und erlogen*). Not a hair of a Jew was disturbed (*den Juden ist kein Haar gekruemmt worden*)."

We looked at one another in amazement. In all our journalistic careers no one among us had experienced anything like it.

Only three minutes from the Wilhelmplatz, on which the Propaganda Ministry was located, was Berlin's famous shopping street, the Leipziger Strasse, at the head of which was Wertheim's internationally known department store, its great show windows broken, its celebrated displays a pile of rubble. Yet Goebbels dared tell us that what we had seen with our own eyes was a "stinking lie."

After a few paralyzing moments we had recovered sufficiently from this shock to want to press Dr. Goebbels with questions. He had disappeared. He had cleverly used the moment of our consternation to eliminate any possibility of our asking him embarassing questions. . . .

"The Past Is Lying in Flames"

The whole civilized world was shocked when on the evening of May 10, 1933, the books of authors displeasing to the Nazis, including even those of our own Helen Keller, were solemnly burned on the immense Franz Joseph Platz between the University of Berlin and the State Opera on Unter den Linden. I was a witness to the scene.

All afternoon Nazi raiding parties had gone into public and private libraries, throwing onto the streets such books as Dr. Goebbels in his supreme wisdom had decided were unfit for Nazi Germany. From the streets Nazi columns of beer-hall fighters had picked up these discarded volumes and taken them to the square above referred to.

Here the heap grew higher and higher, and every few

minutes another howling mob arrived, adding more books to the impressive pyre. Then, as night fell, students from the university, mobilized by the little doctor, performed veritable Indian dances and incantations as the flames began to soar skyward.

When the orgy was at its height, a cavalcade of cars hove into sight. It was the Propaganda Minister himself, accompanied by his bodyguard and a number of fellow torch bearers of the new Nazi *Kultur.*

"Fellow students, German men and women!" he said as he stepped before a microphone for all Germany to hear him. "The age of extreme Jewish intellectualism has now ended, and the success of the German revolution has again given the right of way to the German spirit. . . .

"You are doing the right thing in committing the evil spirit of the past to the flames at this late hour of the night. It is a strong, great, and symbolic act—an act that is to bear witness before all the world to the fact that the spiritual foundation of the November Republic has disappeared. From these ashes there will rise the phoenix of a new spirit. . . .

"The past is lying in flames. The future will rise from the flames within our own hearts. . . . Brightened by these flames our vow shall be: The Reich and the Nation and our Fuehrer Adolf Hitler. *Heil! Heil! Heil!*". . .

The Diaries Reveal Goebbels

What, then, are some of the other characteristics of Goebbels as he reveals himself in his diaries for 1942–43?

Overshadowing all other characteristics was his inordinate ambition. Obsessed with ambition, he became a glutton for work—not because he was overconscientious, but because he was driven on by an almost psychopathic lust for power.

To achieve power he needed to be in the know on what was going on around about him. Accordingly we find him listening by the hour to the gossip of men who could inform him on the foibles and weaknesses of possible rivals. We find him sticking his nose into everything, even in matters which in nowise concerned him.

I could turn to almost any page of his diaries and find him occupying his mind with such matters as potato rations, hair-dos for women in wartime, Nazi terminology in foreign-language dictionaries, griping by the average citizen, requisitioning of copper and pewter ware, the administration of justice, new taxes, houses of ill fame for foreign slave workers, fees for troop entertainers, diet for dancing girls, women in industry, experiments in artificial insemination, itinerary for Countess Ciano, civilian behavior in wartime, character of radio shows, German foreign policy, attitude toward occupied countries, corruption in high places—just to mention a few topics at random.

So ambitious was Goebbels that he refused to take out time for necessary rest. Apparently he feared that by being away from his duties for even a fortnight he might miss something of importance in the determining of which he should have a hand.

He writes about trouble with his nerves, about an itch that has become unbearable, about being very tired and badly in need of rest, about the terrible pain caused by a bad kidney attack, et cetera. Yet such is his ambition and jealous concern for keeping power in his hands that he refuses consistently to heed his doctor's orders to go to Karlsbad for a cure.

Hand in hand with his overweening ambition went a colossal vanity. "The Fuehrer told [Nazi official Albert] Speer he never once discovered a psychological error in my propaganda," he wrote jubilantly on April 24, 1943. "The Fuehrer said if he had a dozen persons like myself he would appoint me," he wrote complacently in connection with filling a post of gauleiter.

Hermann Göring: Hitler's Chosen Successor

Douglas M. Kelley

For five months during 1946, Douglas M. Kelley served as the psychiatrist for the twenty-two Nazi war criminals held at Nuremberg. As part of his responsibilities, he administered medical and psychological tests to the prisoners. He personally interviewed the men and obtained statements from those who were in close contact with the criminals. One of the accused Nazi criminals he interviewed was Hermann Göring. Göring met Hitler during the early days of the Nazi Party and found in him the embodiment of a good leader and a national hero. Hitler believed Göring's aristocratic background and record as an ace pilot during World War I lent authenticity to the Nazi Party. Over the next almost twenty-five years, Hitler and Göring worked side-by-side administering the Third Reich. Hitler elevated Göring to many high-ranking Nazi positions, including Reich marshal and minister of aviation, and chose Göring as his successor.

In this selection from *22 Cells in Nuremberg*, Kelley presents Göring as a shrewd, brilliant and ruthless person. Göring's love of family and of animals, his high intelligence, and charming demeanor seem at odds with his dis-

Douglas M. Kelley, *22 Cells in Nuremberg*. New York: Greenberg, 1947.

regard for human life. Kelley explains that Göring thought of himself not as a war criminal but rather as a brilliant strategist whose final tactic was the taking of his own life prior to his execution.

🐗 🐗 🐗

Of all the Nazis tried at Nuremberg, the one who made the greatest impression, the one who had been in the public eye longest, was Hermann Goering [Göring]. He has been described as almost anything from a Machiavellian villain to a fat, harmless eunuch, the general tendency having been to identify him as a mere satellite of Hitler, who spent his days seeking medals, glory, and riches.

Goering's personality is most important in this discussion since he was the only one of the major Nazis studied. [Heinrich] Himmler and [Paul Joseph] Goebbels, his near co-equal colleagues, and Hitler, his Fuehrer, were already dead. These four individuals were involved in virtually every phase of German government and policy. There is little doubt that they were the nucleus of the Nazi Party. In such effective company there would have been no place for a fat and fatuous fool. And Goering was nobody's fool, not even Hitler's. He was a brilliant, brave, ruthless, grasping, shrewd executive. This opinion of him is the fruit of many hours spent with him in his cell. . . .

A Powerful Figure

Hermann Goering was a man of charming manner (when he chose to be charming), of persuasive speech, and of excellent intelligence bordering on the highest level. In addition, he had a keen imagination and a good educational background. These assets, supplemented by ability as a public speaker, great drive, and a sense of humor, made him Hitler's most outstanding follower. Obviously his complete disregard of human life and his ability to carry out policy no matter how brutal also elevated him in Hitler's eyes.

As a result of his capacities, Goering gained control over more activities than any individual in the Third Reich except Hitler himself. A list of his offices as of April 1, 1945, includes: Hitler's Deputy, Prussian Prime Minister, President of the Prussian State Council, Reich Governor of Prussia, President of the Reichstag, Reich Minister of Aviation, Commander-in-Chief of the Air Force, Reich Forestry and Hunting Master, Chairman of the Ministerial Council for the Defense of the Reich, Member of the Secret Cabinet Council, and Reich Marshal. . . .

As an individual, Goering was one of the most powerful figures in German economics. During a short period as Minister of Economics, he almost completely reorganized this department. He developed the Hermann Goering Works, his combine which grew to be the third largest industrial trust in Europe, controlling huge properties not only in the Reich itself but in conquered or annexed territories.

Unwearied by all his commercial and political and military activities, Goering found ample time to undertake numerous political missions abroad and, while at home, to entertain frequently in grand style at his residences in Germany.

With so much power, Goering was inevitably a target for the envy of most of the other top Nazis. He had recurring disagreements on policy with [Foreign Minister Joachim] von Ribbentrop, Himmler, and others. He developed a special corps of paratroopers to protect him against the "accidents" that might befall a man with such powerful enemies; and, in the end, he had need of his bodyguard. His influence over Hitler gradually weakened during the latter months of the war, primarily as a result of the failure of the Luftwaffe to prevent the wholesale bombing of Germany.

His decline, once it had begun, was hastened by the rivalry and envy of other top Nazis, and he was virtually in retirement during the last few months of the fighting.

An Aggressive Child

Goering's life and his motivations have been as little known as his capacities. His family's love of country was so great that his mother made the long trip from the West Indies to Bavaria so that her son could be born [on January 12, 1893] and brought up on precious German soil. Goering's father, who had been the first governor of the German colony in Southwest Africa and later its minister-president, was at that time consul general in Haiti. Soon after the child was born, Frau Goering returned to her husband and left Hermann with friends in Bavaria. Three years later the family was reunited, when the parents returned to Germany and settled at the Goering estate of Veldenstein in Bavaria.

The lack of early parental authority undoubtedly accounts for the development of some of Goering's aggressiveness and uncontrolled drive. Without a father's or mother's supervision, he did much as he pleased in these first three years, and early established habit traits that are shown later in his inability to conform to authority. His student years were tumultuous, with frequent transfers from one school to another because of his belligerencies toward other children. Finally a proper vent for this aggressive activeness was found in a military school career, with summers spent in vigorous mountain climbing and hunting.

As a result of his military training, Goering entered

the First World War as an officer of infantry. Before the end of 1914, however, he entered the Air Force, and by 1916 was rated one of Germany's major aces. Although shot down and severely wounded in that year, he rejoined his squadron early in 1917 and eventually was made commander of the Richthofen Air Circus, the most famous of the German air units.

At the conclusion of the war, Goering refused to surrender to the Allied forces and flew his entire unit into Germany where they never officially surrendered. For his Air Force exploits, he was awarded the *Pour le Mérite*, Germany's highest military award.

An Early Nazi

After the Armistice, Goering found himself without special peacetime skill or training. Jobless, he felt a deep sense of frustration in Germany's defeat. In addition, he was possessed of tremendous energy and deep aggressive drives for which he had no ready outlet. He spent his energies protesting ineffectually against various Allied activities in Germany and in traveling about seeking a job. Finally he went to Sweden and worked in an aircraft plant. In Sweden he courted a married woman, the Baroness Karin von Faulk, and after she had obtained a divorce married her and returned to Germany to live near Munich. There, conscious of the meagerness of his education, he attended the University of Munich for the next year, taking courses in history and political science.

During this period, Goering met Hitler and became an enthusiastic Nazi Party member. When I asked him whether it was Hitler's oratory or his arguments that won him over, Goering insisted that it was neither but rather eagerness on his part for personal aggrandizement. "I hated the Republic," he said. "I knew it could not last. I saw that as soon as the Allies withdrew their support, a new government would take over Germany. I wanted to help destroy the Republic and to be, perhaps, the ruler of the new Reich.". . .

A Drug Addict

In any event, Goering soon became a big man in the little party [National Socialist Party]. He formed the Storm Troops for Hitler, and he was one of the major leaders in the Munich Putsch of 1923. In this action he was wounded in the right thigh and later developed a severe infection which caused him to be hospitalized until 1924. While suffering from this wound, he was given considerable amounts of narcotics and developed a morphine addiction. . . .

A side of Goering's personality which is little known was his extreme fondness for and tenderness toward his family and friends. His abilities as a host have been publicized, and there is little doubt that he genuinely enjoyed giving rollicking parties for those of whom he was fond. Easily swayed emotionally, he put all his great drive and enthusiasm into his current relationships. For him it was the present that counted, a present lighted by the rosy dawn of an always better future. . . .

Goering was not impotent nor was he, as persistent rumors implied, a homosexual. He naturally denied any perversions, and psychiatric observation and independent conversations with other prisoners who had known Goering well seemed to bear him out. He probably sublimated his sex drive into hard work, which gave him his amazing ability to keep going eighteen hours a day. Undoubtedly ambition took precedence over "amour." However, his home life was a happy one, and the devotion between Goering and his second wife [Emmy Sonnemann, whom he married in 1934 and with whom he had a daughter in 1938] seemed satisfying to both.

Aside from his own future, Goering's primary concern in jail seemed to be for his family. He once told me that, on his surrender, the only condition he asked was that his family be adequately cared for. His letters to his wife and child indicate not only his strong love, but his effervescent emotions. . . .

Goering carried this tenderness of feeling into another sphere. Although he himself was a great hunter, he loved animals and felt that they should be protected. For that purpose, he drew up the Reich hunting and forestry laws. For these creatures, for his friends, for his family, nothing was too good. Beyond this circle his interest in any other living thing amounted to almost total disregard. . . .

Of Value to the Party

That is the Goering who ordered the bombing of Rotterdam, the man who said to me: "Of course, we rearmed. We rearmed Germany until we bristled. I am only sorry we did not rearm more. Of course, I considered treaties as so much toilet paper. Of course, I wanted to make Germany great. If it could be done peacefully, well and good. If not, that's just as good. My plans against Britain were bigger than they ascribe even now. When they told me I was playing with war by building up the Luftwaffe, I replied I certainly was not running a finishing school.

"I joined the Party because it was revolutionary, not because of the ideological stuff. Other parties have made revolutions, so I figured I could get in on one too; and the thing that attracted me to the Nazi Party was that it was the only one that had the guts to say 'to hell with Versailles,' while the others were smiling and appeasing. That's what got me. Naturally, Hitler was glad to have me because I had a great reputation among officers of the First World War. I was of value, and in turn I was to become leader of the Reich.". . .

Charming Yet Ruthless

Charming as Hermann Goering unquestionably was—when, as a prisoner in our hands, it suited him to be so—his own fascinating conversation made it unmistakably clear that he had no sense whatsoever of the value of human life, of moral obligation, or of the other finer attributes of civilized man when they conflicted with his own egocentric aims. He was an individual who one moment could be the life of the party and a friend to all and the next could, without compunction, order all his companions to their deaths. . . .

Nonetheless, no matter how much we disapprove of Goering's ruthless disregard for human life, we must recognize his tremendous drive and capacity for work which, coupled with keen intelligence, made him Hitler's most valuable executive. He lost favor only because the war was lost.

Goering's final days as a member of the Third Reich reveal how completely his jealous rivals within the Party had influenced Hitler. On April 22, 1945, Hitler had a discussion with [Alfred] Jodl, his commander-in-chief, in which he announced his intended suicide and told Jodl that Goering would assume the Fuehrership. When Hitler also notified Eva Braun, still his mistress, of this decision, Jodl was convinced. He sent word to Goering that Hitler planned to remain in Berlin to the last, but that the end was near, and Goering was to take command on Hitler's death.

Goering received Jodl's message late that evening and the next morning wired Hitler requesting further information and the specific date on which he was to assume command. Goering did not know that, after announcing his plans to Jodl and notifying Eva, Hitler had changed his mind. Hitler was not told that Jodl had communicated with Goering and was led to view Goering's telegram as a move to usurp power.

I questioned Ribbentrop as well as Jodl on this point. Ribbentrop had been with Hitler at the time and he verified all Goering told me. But he swore that it was the consensus of all the leaders then in Berlin—[Martin] Bormann (successor to [Rudolf] Hess), Goebbels, and Ribbentrop himself (Jodl having returned to the field)—that Goering was simply trying to take over the government. Apparently those three, who were all bitter rivals of Goering, joined to convince Hitler of Goering's duplicity.

Apparently this took some doing, though; for at six o'clock on the evening of the twenty-third Hitler wired Goering that the date had not yet been set but that Goering would be duly notified. Goering, elated, planned a celebration which would mark the achievement of his great dream—empty as it was by then. The party never took place. At eight o'clock the same evening a group of SS troops arrived and put him under house arrest. Their orders read that he had acted in a treasonable fashion toward Hitler and the Party, but that Hitler had ordered his life spared because of his previous great work in the Third Reich.

Goering spent the next four days under house arrest, and on April 27 he received an unsigned telegram informing him that he had been ousted from the Party. On the night of April 29 another telegram arrived, signed Bormann, with direct orders for the SS to liquidate Goering and his staff. But the Gestapo chief, [Ernst] Kaltenbrunner, was reluctant to have Goering shot without having Hitler's signature on the order. He delayed, and Goering lived.

There is little doubt in the minds of everyone concerned with this affair that Hitler probably never saw the Bormann telegram and that it was conceived and sent by Bormann and Goebbels. By May 2, Goering had completed plans for his liberation. At three o'clock that afternoon a number of Luftwaffe paratroopers passed through the grounds of Goering's castle and "by coincidence" the lead truck of the convoy broke down. The paratroopers all got out to stretch their legs and suddenly surrounded Goering's guards. As simply as that Goering was again a free man.

The rescue maneuver, while spectacular, was hardly worth while, for at eight o'clock that evening an order from [Albert] Kesselring, commander of the area, arrived, officially ordering Goering's release. Twice freed, he remained in his castle until a week later when he surrenderd to the American Army.

Goering's surrender was typical. He arrived laden with jewelry, joy, and a trunkful of paracodeine pills—the entire German stock of the drug; and since the drug was unknown outside Germany, that means the entire world supply of paracodeine. He greeted his captors jovially, accepted the Army's contention that he was a prisoner of war, and gladly surrendered his valuable baton, the symbol of his marshalship. . . .

A Natural Leader

Goering's fondness for the finest in everything applied not only to his personal possessions but to his dwellings. He maintained a number of castles which he had furnished with some of Europe's finest art. And he apparently knew the merit of his paintings. His collectors have stated that his knowledge of art was not at all superficial but rather that of a seasoned and intelligent connoisseur.

Most of the art Goering looted had been recovered before I left Nuremberg. When I asked him why he took paintings, tapestries, and sculpture on so magnificent a scale, he assured me: "I had no intention of keeping them for myself. Always I thought of Germany. I made plans that on my death a huge museum would be

created for the German people." He paused and cast
me a proud side glance. "Naturally, the great gift would
be known as the Hermann Goering Collection.". . .

Moreover, he was a natural leader. When the trial began he demonstrated his peculiar abilities of leadership
immediately by assuming his place at the head of the
dining table. No one questioned this. His right to command was apparently taken for granted by all of the
prisoners, and thereafter Goering fancied himself as
leader in the defense of his compatriots. He said to me:
"We are sort of like a team, all of us who have been accused, and it is up to us to stick together to accomplish
the strongest, defense. Naturally, I am the leader, so it
is my problem to see that each of us contributes his
share.". . .

As distinctive as Goering's natural assumption of
leadership was his ability to disregard those aspects of
the circumstances which denied or belittled his authority. The sudden change of environment from a situation wherein his slightest wish was immediately granted
to incarceration in a tiny cell containing only a bed, a
table, a chair, and a toilet, must have been profoundly
shocking, and yet Goering probably complained less
and accepted prison routine with more grace than almost any other of the group.

He was a man of big ideas, massive plans. Even in
prison, he remained primarily concerned with fundamental issues, and the petty problems of daily prison
life he simply shrugged away. What complaints he
made were about lack of communication with his wife.
Once he was able to send and receive letters regularly,
he settled back and became a nearly model prisoner.
This ability to adapt himself to sudden change was one
of Goering's primary assets. His simple interest in the
end point, rather than in the situation as it developed,
had been characteristic of him throughout his life.

For a Greater Germany

At Nuremberg, Goering assumed that he would be found guilty and condemned to death. He accepted this fate—maintaining constantly that he was being punished as a German patriot rather than as a war criminal—and throughout the trial concerned himself with keeping his name as free as possible from the taint of atrocities and war crimes.

So far as the organization of the Party and the plans for war were concerned, Goering from the first willingly admitted his part to me. In the trial, and to me on occasion, he stressed that he did what he did only to build a greater Germany, not for his own personal aggrandizement. In intimate talks on the bunk in his cell, however, he sometimes confessed that his basic motive had been that single, driving ambition—to achieve for Hermann Goering supreme command of the Third Reich. . . .

He did not lose hope or even ambition for posthumous glory and power. His sole aim became to establish himself in the minds of the German people in such a way that he would go down in the history of his country as one of its great heroes. Time and again he said to me boastfully: "Yes, I know I shall hang. You know I shall hang. I am ready. But I am determined to go down in German history as a great man. If I cannot convince the court, I shall at least convince the German people that all I did was done for the Greater German Reich. In fifty or sixty years there will be statues of Hermann Goering all over Germany. Little statues, maybe, but one in every German home."

In spite of the grind of prison life, Goering's moods were usually good and he loved to tell jokes, most of which were not very funny but which he always enjoyed, regardless of their effect on anyone else. . . .

In the intimacy of his cell, Goering talked freely and apparently honestly of his relations with Hitler. He admitted that he had had many differences with Hitler and that, as time went on, their arguments became more and more serious. He pointed out that he was the only one who dared argue directly with Hitler during the war years and explained that these arguments eventually led to Hitler's distrust of him. Everyone else, he agreed, used to accept unquestioningly whatever Hitler said. When I remarked that in America all of Hitler's followers, including Goering, were considered "yes-men," Goering nodded understandingly. "That may well be, but please show me a 'no-man' in Germany who is not six feet underground today."

Goering apparently had a close attachment to Hitler—but a curious one. His was no deep, unreasoned love for his Fuehrer, but a cool, intellectual admiration for Hitler's organizational capacity and his uncanny ability to control people en masse. . . .

Goering had only contempt for most of his colleagues, and he would have been quite willing to convict all of them of the most heinous offenses if by so doing he could have vindicated himself.

"Brilliant Strategy"

Goering's whole aim, from the time he surrendered, was to build up Hermann Goering for posterity. He even tried hard at one point to convince me that if he had been given a free hand he could have re-established his Luftwaffe, and perhaps the Germans might have won the race for the development of the atom bomb. . . .

Goering never felt that he was a war criminal, and he challenged the right of any tribunal to try him. He actually never felt that what we called war crimes were criminal at all. He simply called them "brilliant strategy."

But Goering was not afraid to die for his strategy. "What is there to be afraid of?" he once asked me. "After I have given orders to hundreds of thousands of men to go into battle, frequently knowing full well that many would not come back, plain soldiers who had no choice in the matter, should I, their leader, cringe when called on to face the enemy? . . .

"Hermann Goering is a soldier. I made war—that is true. As long as every nation has its selfish interests, you have to be practical. I am a practical man."

He stopped for a moment and looked around his cell. It seemed he was realizing that "practical" men avoid such ends as this rough prison and the gallows. He went on: "But I am also convinced that there is a higher power which pushes men around in spite of all of their efforts to control their destiny. . . ."

That was the only time I ever saw Goering realize that he alone could not face and perhaps conquer the entire world.

Thus, in his prison cell, Goering demonstrated all of those personality characteristics which have made him what he was throughout his life. He still maintained his extroverted reaction patterns, his need for attention, his narcissistic bodily fixations. He daily demonstrated, though restricted by the prison environment, his dominant drives, his ability to visualize clearly his goal, and his willingness to attain his end regardless of the cost. He still possessed all the forcefulness, brutality, ruthlessness and lack of conscience which made him the ideal executive for Adolf Hitler in the control of the Third Reich.

Death by His Own Hand

In his . . . suicide [by poison on October 15, 1946] Goering carried out his ideals to the very end. He had faced the International Tribunal with courage but denied its right to judge or sentence him. In his last moments of life, he took matters into his own hands and, once again the dominant figure, cheated the hangman of the Allied nations.

Heinrich Himmler: Mass Murderer

Joachim C. Fest

There was nothing in Heinrich Himmler's background to suggest he was capable of the atrocities he committed while a leader in Nazi Germany. As a student of agriculture, one of Himmler's first jobs was as a fertilizer salesman. He left his job in 1923 to join the Nazi Party and was present as a flag bearer during the failed Beer Hall Putsch. He went on to become leader of the Schutzstaffel (SS), Hitler's elite bodyguards; and the secret state police, the Gestapo. He also created and directed the concentration camps at which millions were exterminated. In this excerpt from *The Face of the Third Reich: Portraits of the Nazi Leadership*, Joachim C. Fest portrays Himmler as an insecure and emotionless man whose fanatical personality would not allow him regard for human life. Fest also discusses Himmler's requirements for the "man of violence" he needed to commit mass murder and extermination. Fest shows Himmler to be a colorless character whose deep-seated need for security expressed itself in the adoration of Adolf Hitler.

Fest was born in Berlin in 1926. After World War II he became head of the Department of Contemporary History for a radio station in the American area of Berlin. *The Face of the Third Reich* originated from a series of broadcasts about German history that Fest wrote in the 1960s. His other books include *Hitler* and *Plotting Hitler's Death: The Story of German Resistance.*

🐝 🐝 🐝

[H]einrich Himmler,] the man who wrote some of the most terrible chapters in German history was born in Munich on October 7, 1900. His family atmosphere and all the main impressions of his years of development were evidently decisively influenced by the personality of his father, who, as the son of a police president, a former tutor to the princes at the Bavarian court and a headmaster, also applied authoritarian principles in his own household. . . . His opposition to his father's discipline and upbringing may have engendered a kind of dependence that later expressed itself as a complex need to look up to someone and surrender himself to that person. His fanatical concern with education, which led him continually to try to teach and impart axioms for living, was doubtless also largely the outcome of his early years. The doctor Felix Kersten, who treated him continuously from 1939 onwards and enjoyed his confidence, has asserted that Himmler himself would rather have educated foreign peoples than exterminate them. During the war [World War II] he spoke enthusiastically—looking ahead to peace—of establishing military units who were 'educated and trained, once education and training can be practised again'.

A Born Organizer

It was at first intended that Himmler should become a farmer, and this was the source of the peasant ideas which later infused his ideological conceptions, especially in relation to the SS. But his poor physical constitution would in any case have made him unfit for a farmer's life. . . . [Himmler] described himself as 'a peasant by ancestry, blood and nature'. But after the First World War, in which he had taken part at the very end as an ensign, he came via a rightist-radical soldiers' association to Hitler's party. A photograph of the November Putsch of 1923 shows him as a standard-bearer at the side of Ernst Röhm. Soon he emerged as a colleague of [Nazi Party Organizer] Gregor Strasser in the social-revolutionary wing of the NSDAP [the Nazi Party]; undoubtedly this association sprang not so much from ideological motives as from the fact that he and Strasser were compatriots. In fact his ideological position, which later seemed so resolute, remained for a long time vague and indefinite. In 1926 he met Margarete Boden, the daughter of a West Prussian landowner. She had served as a nurse in the war and later had built up a modest private nursing home with her father's money. She was seven years older than Himmler, fair-haired and blue-eyed in complete conformity with the supposed Germanic type. Two years later he married her, and it was she, it was revealed later, who aroused his interest in homeopathy, mesmerism, oat-straw baths and herbalism.

On January 6, 1929 Himmler, at the same time running a chicken farm at Waldtrudering near Munich, was appointed head of the then barely three-hundred-man-strong SS. He proved his abilities as an organiser by expanding the force to over 50,000 men by 1933. He was still a marginal figure in the top leadership; it was only during the seizure of power that, along with his superior assistant Reinhard Heydrich, he methodically and patiently worked his way up and gained control of the Political Police. June 30, 1934 [the Night of Long Knives, when Hitler liquidated many members of the Sturmabteilung or SA] was the crucial day of his career. After he had worked in the background on the construction of the scenery before which the clumsy [SA leader Ernst] Röhm, for whom he had once carried the banner, advanced to his own execution, his SS units provided the murder commandos for the three-day massacre. From the rivalry between the Reichswehr [armed resistance] and the SA he emerged alongside Hitler as the true victor. Only three weeks later the SS, hitherto subordinate to the SA, was raised to the status of an independent organisation. When on June 17, 1936 Himmler was finally appointed head of the now unified police forces of the Reich and confirmed as Reichsführer of the SS, he seemed to have reached the peak of an astounding career. He now controlled a substantial portion of the real power and also, thanks to the terror that he spread, an even greater part of the psychological power.

This appointment provided him, in fact, with a springboard for a process of expansion which largely determined the future face and history of the Third Reich, and in the course of which the real power visibly shifted towards himself and the SS. What he had been secretly preparing for a long time, egged on by Heydrich restlessly working in the background, now took shape step by step as the conquest of positions of solid power. [Under Himmler's authority,] the SS mobile troops, the economic and administrative head office of the SS, the concentration camps, the SS security service, the Head Office for Race and Settlement, and finally the Waffen SS soon grew from small institutions with limited functions into powerful organisations. . . .

[After the attempted revolt of July 20, 1944] the SS now pushed its way into the centre of the organisational fabric of the Wehrmacht' [German Army], and Himmler, who had meanwhile also become Reich Minister of the Interior, now in addition became chief of the Replacement Army. On top of his many other functions he was thus in charge 'of all military transport, military censorship, the intelligence service, surveillance of the troops, the supply of food, clothing and pay to the troops, and care of the wounded'.

Within this picture of consistent and soberly planned extensions of power, individual eccentricities were not lacking. While the majority of Himmler's organisations, foundations and acquisitions served realistic power aims, others merely satisfied his private fantasies—like the Mattoni mineral-water factory, the Lebensborn eV (the state-registered organisation for the promotion of human propagation), the Nordland Publishing Company, the cultivation of Kog-Sagy's roots, or the SS Association for Research and Teaching on Heredity, whose task it was 'to investigate the geographical distribution, spirit, deeds and heritage of the Nordic Indo-Germanic race'.

Himmler Institutes Terrorism as an Institution

Himmler's comprehensive and unitary organisation provided the totalitarian government with the systematic control that now enabled it to operate to its full extent. No sooner had Himmler, in the course of capturing power, seized control of the police than a perceptible tightening of the regime could be felt. The spontaneous acts of violence that had marked the initial phases of the Third Reich lessened and then ceased altogether with the final removal of power from the SA. The 'emotional' terrorism practised by Ernst Röhm's shock troops with a blend of political and criminal techniques gave way to its rational counterpart, a central bureaucracy systematically employing terrorism as an institution. The new type of man of violence recruited by Himmler was concerned with the dispassionate extermination of real or possible opponents, not with the primitive release of sadistic impulses. Whatever sadism occurred, particularly in the concentration camps, was included by Himmler among those 'exceptional cases of human weakness' of which he had spoken in his [October 4, 1943] Poznan speech . . . [to SS group leaders]; they occurred in contradiction of the 'idea' of the type. His perpetually reiterated moral admonishments are in no way a merely feigned moral austerity not 'meant seriously'; they are founded in the principle of rational terrorism. He took ruthless measures in cases where corruption, brutality or any other personal motives were apparent, and even trusted henchmen were not spared. . . .

The Most Extreme SS Man of the Führer's Followers

[It was] the vulgar and calculating pride in his own capacity for inhumanity with which the pedant and the former model pupil of the King Wilhelm Gymnasium in Munich sought to establish his leadership among his murder-and-battle-hardened subordinates. In fact it is difficult even now to understand to what individual qualities and advantages he owed his relatively uncontested position within the SS. He was the most colourless personality in the inner circle of the leaders of the Third Reich; he possessed no natural authority and his 'charisma' was that of a head teacher. The long years of screening by Heydrich, and Hitler's personal trust, which lasted to the end and which he paid for with extreme docility, clearly assisted him greatly. In addition, the Order's stringent principles of obedience and duty helped to keep his position uncontested, and its members were always being involved in new tasks imposed by its continuous expansionist drive, which gave them sufficient goals to exercise their rivalry outside the SS. But independently of this, he himself was always concerned to reinforce his influence, not merely institutionally but also psychologically, by proving both to those above him and those below him that he was the most extreme SS man among the Führer's followers. Indeed, totalitarian systems in general owe their inhumanity more to competition between rivals jealously striving for power than to the principle of contempt for human beings as such.

It is true that from the time when the SS became more and more exclusively engaged in mass murder and extermination, Himmler's extremist protestations frequently took on strained undertones. 'We must forswear and renounce false comradeship, falsely conceived compassion, false softness, and a false excuse to ourselves', he once cried out almost passionately to his listeners. The observation that in his purposeful coldness he was beyond reach of all feeling is undoubtedly correct. All feelings of guilt, of individual responsibility, were warded off and 'dealt with' partly by his pseudo-moral values, partly by interposing those bureaucratic mechanisms that gave his character its specific stamp, so that they did not reach the foundations of his personality. Nevertheless we may surmise that the ever louder admonishments to harshness and ruthlessness were intended to drown elements of unrest which in the end he could not fail to hear. The scope of the terrorist activity made it inevitable that occasionally he should face the consequences of what he had thoughtlessly set in motion at the conference table or by putting his signature to documents. But he himself did not have the hardness he demanded from his subordinates, any more than he had the rest of the élite characteristics of the SS man, the external racial features, the physical height, the hair colour, or the so-called Great Family Tree (*Grosse Ahnennachweis*) going back to 1750. There is no evidence that he was conscious of these problems or suffered from them. Only once does he seem to have submitted himself to the sight of what he demanded from others. SS Obergruppenführer von dem Bach-Zelewski has attested that in 1941 in Minsk, Himmler ordered a hundred prisoners to be assembled for a model execution. At the first salvo, however, he almost fainted, and he screamed when the execution squad failed to kill two women outright. In significant contrast to his abstract readiness to commit murder was the heartfelt emotion, described elsewhere, which overcame him at the sight of blond children, and his positively hysterical opposition to hunting. His lunch was ruined if he was reminded that animals had been slaughtered. . . .

Himmler's Utopian Fanaticism

The almost incomprehensible distortion of all standards of judgment revealed when this observation is set beside what he said about experiments on living prisoners or the 'treatment of other races in the East' can be understood only in the context of his utopian fanaticism, which in its narrow-minded obsessionalism undoubtedly contained an element of insanity, and in the context of his world of ideas that was totally divorced from human reality. At an early stage he had shown that he could attribute idealistic motives to his behaviour. In 1921, when he was active in student self-government, he wrote in his diary: 'In actual fact I did not originally do it for idealistic reasons. Now that I have done it, I shall do it idealistically'. This ability to make 'decent' motives seem plausible according to changing needs prepared the way for a further abstraction of all activity from categories of individual guilt and made possible, not only for him but for a large number of his subordinates, a clouding of all personal responsibility. The human experiments in the laboratories of the concentration camps, which displayed a horrifying amateurism, yielded not the slightest useful result because their real purpose was merely to act as a blind; in the words of one of the doctors involved, Himmler wanted to prove 'that he was not a murderer but a patron of science'. Any remaining feelings of guilt were removed by the assertion, delivered with the pseudo-tragic pose of provincial demonism, that it was 'the curse of the great to have to walk over corpses'. Behind this, conjured up more zealously than ever, lay that concept of a Greater German postwar empire which, beyond the extermination which he carried out with routine conscientiousness, he was planning and preparing. The nature of these plans is disclosed by the terms in which he expressed himself on this 'theme of his life', by means of which he hoped to escape from the constraints of his dry and colourless existence to a position of leadership in idealised territories. '*Herrenmenschen*' [gentlemen] were contrasted with 'working peoples'; there was talk of 'fields of racial experiment', 'nordification', 'aids to procreation', 'the foundations of our blood', 'fundamental biological laws', 'the ruination of our blood', 'the breeding of a new human type', or 'the botanical garden of Germanic blood'—truly the visions of a poultry farmer from Wald trudering! Meanwhile Himmler devised plans for an SS State of Burgundy, which was to enjoy a certain autonomy as a racially and ideologically model state under his personal leadership, to be a sort of gigantic Nordic boarding school; this idea gave his narrow-minded pedagogic temperament the cold happiness for which it longed. As it has been said of the spokesmen of the French Revolution that they confused politics with a novel, so it may be said of Himmler that he confused politics with the obscure and fanciful tracts that had been the first stage in the educational career of his Führer.

Devotion to Hitler

The ultimate indissoluble residue of Himmler's make-up rests upon his devotion to the person of Hitler, to whom he subordinated himself in a positively pathological manner. His dependent nature and need of emotional support, demonstrated both by his choice of a wife seven years older than himself and by the dogmatic pedantry of his beliefs, culminated in an exaggerated loyalty towards the 'Führer of the Greater Germanic Reich', as he liked to call Hitler in anticipation of the future. Once when [his doctor] Felix Kersten was treating Himmler, Kersten answered the telephone; Himmler turned to him, his eyes shining, and said, 'You have been listening to the voice of the Führer, you're a very lucky man'. The head of the German Intelligence Service, Walter Schellenberg, who was his adviser towards the end of the war, reports that after every conversation with his Führer, Himmler used to imitate his speech and mode of expression. Kersten says that Himmler saw in Hitler's orders 'the binding decisions of the Germanic race's Führer, pronouncements from a world transcending this one', which 'possessed a divine power':

> He [Hitler] rose up out of our deepest need, when the German people had come to a dead end. He is one of those brilliant figures which always appear in the Germanic world when it has reached a final crisis in body, mind and soul. [Writer Johann von] Goethe was one such figure in the intellectual sphere, [Chancellor Otto von] Bismarck in the political—the Führer in the political, cultural and military combined. It has been ordained by the Karma of the Germanic world that he should wage war against the East and save the Germanic peoples—a figure of the greatest brilliance has become incarnate in his person.

Kersten himself adds: 'Himmler uttered these words with great solemnity and effect. Now it became clear to me why Himmler had sometimes pointed to Hitler as a person whom men would regard in centuries to come with the same reverence that they accorded to Christ'.

If the devoutly exaggerated absoluteness of his loyalty towards the Führer-god corresponded to a deep need on Himmler's part for security and something to hold on to, it is also understandable that his faith barely stood up to the strain of the final phase of the regime. For when, with the turn of the tide in the war and Hitler's increasingly obvious failure, the first cracks and fissures began to show on the idol, he instantly relapsed into his fundamental vacillation. Today we may take it as proved that from 1943 onwards he had loose, informative contacts with the Resistance Movement and even played a still unclarified but unquestionably dubious role in the events of July 20 [the 1944 assassination attempt] before entering in the spring of 1945 into secret negotiations with a representative of the World Jewish Congress and finally with Count Folke Bernadotte. In so far as he was not forced into these negotiations against his will it remains questionable whether he ever intended to commit an act of conscious disloyalty. It is more probable that in a corner of his pathologically adoring heart he maintained the altars of his idol-worship to the last and that this was why his actions were irresolute and unplanned. But the inherent weight of the enormous power which he had gathered together during the last few years—not least with an eye on the succession to Hitler—now forced him to act.

Himmler Betrays Hitler

The steps he took, however, indicate an almost incredible divorce from reality. He greeted the representative of the World Jewish Congress, who came to see him on April 21, 1945, with the unbelievable words: "Welcome to Germany, Herr Masur. It is time you Jews and we National Socialists buried the hatchet". He indulged in speculation upon what he would do as soon as he came to power, and seriously hoped, up to the day of his arrest, that the Western Allies would greet him as a partner in negotiations and even as an ally against Soviet

Russia. When he visited Grand Admiral [Karl] Dönitz, who had just been appointed Hitler's successor, on May 1, he spoke of his "widespread reputation" abroad. Having bid farewell to Dönitz he was still planning on May 5 to create a National Socialist government under his personal leadership in Schleswig-Holstein, to provide him with the legal right to negotiate with the Western Allies.

In the last analysis it was this stupendous lack of realism which determined this man's life and character. Once, in the panic turbulence of those days when, after shattered hopes, he became aware of reality in the shape of the approaching disaster, he told one of his colleagues, 'I shudder at the thought of everything that is going to happen now'. And if it was only fear that he felt now, this too was something he had obviously never considered, because it had never appeared either in documents or reports, or in his daydreams of future projects. They did not mention the fact that man is afraid of death.

Indeed, during these weeks of the collapse of the Third Reich the SS Reichsführer Heinrich Himmler was an opportunist fighting stubbornly to delay the end. In vain did those around him press him to declare himself and assume responsibility for the SS. On March 19 he was still conjuring up apocalyptic visions of a last-ditch stand to the last man 'like the Ostrogoths on Vesuvius'; now he thought only of disguise and flight. 'One thing can never be forgiven among us Germans: that is treachery', he had assured his followers a few months earlier. No small number of the SS, especially members of the élite groups, committed suicide when they realised Heinrich Himmler's treachery. In Bohemia, in May 1945, according to a contemporary report, SS officers lit a fire one night, stood in a circle around it singing the SS oath song 'Wenn alle untreu werden'

(When all become untrue), and thereafter all took their own lives. What caused their disillusionment so suddenly and with such shock was not so much the betrayal to which Hitler was referring when he repudiated Himmler in his testament and stripped him of all his offices because of his independent peace feelers with the Western powers. In so far as their motives related to the SS leader's actions, it was rather his betrayal of the shared 'idea of the SS', in which they had believed through all battles, all victories, defeats, and crimes. Its collapse left only a senseless, filthy, barbaric murder industry, for which there could be no defence. Rudolf Höss, for many years commandant of Auschwitz, became 'quite mute' when Himmler, 'radiant and in the best of spirits', advised him to go underground.

Evidently the mechanism that produced illusion did not break down even now. On May 21, 1945, when Himmler left Flensburg under the name of Heinrich Hitzinger, his moustache shaved off and a black patch over his left eye, he had chosen for his disguise the uniform of a sergeant-major of the Secret Military Police, a subdivision of the Gestapo. Not grasping the terrifying reputation of all organisations associated with his name, he had no idea that he had thereby laid himself open to automatic arrest. The very same day he was taken prisoner by a British control post.

He put an appropriate end to his life. Suicide erased whatever justification he had advanced for the sufferings he had caused. 'My behaviour is more important than what I say', he had declared in his Poznan speech, and added, 'This Germanic Reich needs the Order of the SS. It needs it at least for the next few centuries'. Now his behaviour contradicted it all. There is no legend.

Rudolf Hess: Hitler's Personal Secretary

Alfred D. Low

Rudolf D. Hess was a student at the University of Munich when he met Hitler. Already a member of the Nazi Party at the time of the Beer Hall Putsch in 1923, Hess was imprisoned for two years because of his participation in that revolt. Hitler's and Hess's simultaneous incarceration brought the two close together, and Hess spent long hours with Hitler helping him write *Mein Kampf*. In the following excerpt from *The Men Around Hitler: The Nazi Elite and Its Collaborators*, Alfred D. Low points out that long before he met Hitler, Hess was searching for a dictator to unify Germany and fight what he perceived to be the power of the Jews. After meeting Hitler, Hess abandoned a career as a scholar to work for the Nazi leader. Although Hess held many high-ranking Nazi positions, he is probably best known for his May 10, 1941, flight to Scotland in search of peace with England. Many thought Hess insane because of his incoherent ramblings at the Nuremberg trials, but Low's research illustrates that Hess was sane. He was sentenced to life in prison and is often called "the Last Nazi" because he was the last of Hitler's henchmen to die; he lived to the age of ninety-three.

Low is professor emeritus of history at Marquette University in Milwaukee, Wisconsin, and was director of its Institute of German Affairs. He is also the author of *The Anschluss Movement, 1931–1938, and the Great Powers* and *Soviet Jewry and Soviet Policy.*

❦   ❦   ❦

Rudolf Hess was born in 1893 in Alexandria, Egypt, where his father was a wholesale merchant. His mother, Klara Muench, was a native of Bavaria. For six years he attended a German school in Alexandria and was sent thereafter to a high school in Switzerland and then to Godesberg, Germany. He was jeered by his schoolmates for being born abroad and not being a "true" German, but was liked by his teachers. He served an apprenticeship in business in Hamburg. . . .

When [World War I] broke out, he volunteered for the *Schweren Reiter* [cavalry] but was admitted only to the Reserve. He participated in World War I serving during its entire length. In 1915–16 he still believed that Germany would achieve final victory through many little victories on different fronts. He showed bitterness toward England, and the U.S., which lined up against Germany. Later the unexpected retreat in the West and the "humiliating" armistice and their climax, the November Revolution affected Hess deeply and caused bitter disappointment. As many Germans, he blamed individuals and various groups—leftist radicals, Independent Socialist, [and] Workers and—as well as Jews for the military debacle and the Western Allies for the harsh stipulations of the peace treaties of Versailles and St. Germain.

His political development was perhaps slow. He wavered a long time before deciding on a political rather than on an academic career. He was 25 years old when he met Dr. Karl Haushofer, Professor of Geography and Geopolitics at the University of Munich, a noted scholar, prolific writer, and world traveler who became a fatherly friend. Hess joined the Thule Society which preached a potpourri of racial selectivity, Germany's resurgence as a world power, and occultism. In his view, "our Jewish press" opposed a foreign policy link of Germany with Soviet Russia—which Hess favored at the moment—since then the Jewish capitalists would lose business, a judgment totally ignoring British and French conditions. While embracing Hitler's conception of an ideal society, he agreed with him that first a "dictator" would have to emerge to unify the Germans and fight the *Judenwirtschaft* (unsavory Jewish power) and Jewish "shoving and profiteering" (*Schieberei und Wucherei*).

It was hardly surprising that Hess embraced in the 1920s other facets of Nazi philosophy, the contemptuous attitude toward the bourgeoisie, racist nationalism, anti-feminism, the unbounded admiration for the Führer, and belief in the inevitable conflict between Great Britain and America—developed by the Führer in a second posthumous publication in which he voiced the view that Germany would take England's side. Though Hess and Hitler had quite a different view of their self-importance—Hitler never doubting it and Hess being rather modest and insecure—they had much in common. As *Frontkämpfer* [soldiers on the front lines] they had been active participants in the war and had both been wounded. Neither had obtained officer's rank and neither could forget the war and its sacrifices. Both were infuriated that the war had been lost and were frantically searching for a scapegoat for the undeserved defeat, castigating leftists and Jews and angrily disputing those who declared the war "senseless." Hess was ready to use brutal Nazi methods of fighting the domestic enemy, comparing their struggle with the

Soviets' "criminal" behavior of smashing the opposition. The Nazi struggle, however, was justified.

The Academician vs. the Politician

For a long time Hess wavered between an academic career and full devotion to politics. In a letter of October 24, 1923, to Ilse Prönl, who later became his wife, the 29-year-old revealed indecisiveness and ambivalence between the need for quiet work and retreat from belligerent politics and his longing for culture and Mozart, for the piano and the flute. He disclosed that he did not understand himself.

Though he participated in the November *Putsch* of 1923—he was instructed to arrest the Bavarian Ministers but was unable to prevent their escape—he hardly covered himself with glory. He fled to Austria, vanishing for several months, while actually studying and engaging in winter sports. Only several months later he surrendered to German authorities, thinking, as he wrote to his mother, that if arrested later, it might be at a less convenient time. He had also heard that in prison he could "study quietly," have "interesting company," good food, separate sleeping facilities, and a "beautiful view."

At Landsberg Hess was daily together with Adolf Hitler, "a wonderful (*prächtig*) human being." Both he and Hitler, he reported, enjoyed the "friendly restfulness" of the prison and the many visitors, including General Erich Ludendorff. In Landsberg Hitler wrote *Mein Kampf* and Hess assisted him, carefully listening to his reading aloud various chapters and editing them. He became enamored of the Führer, "our tribune," and praised his manifold interests, besides politics, art and architecture. Hitler, he wrote, had gained his viewpoint on the Jewish question "after the most difficult inner struggle," always being plagued by doubts that he would not "act unjustly." On one occasion the two men, Hitler sobbing and Hess tearful, cried over the struggle and the sufferings of their people and were enraged about "the treason" which allegedly had caused it all. Hitler pledged to one day take vengeance in the name of the fallen soldiers. What linked them at the moment was the unwillingness to forget the past, the war victims, and the desire for revenge against allegedly guilty individuals and groups.

Rudolf Hess

It was in Landsberg that, after having mutually bared their souls, Hess virtually surrendered to Hitler: "I am dedicated to him more than ever. I love him." Hess finally abandoned his thoughts of a scholarly career to which he was inclined, and accepted Hitler's offer to serve him. His decision may have been made easier since the remuneration offered was twice as large as that paid by Dr. Haushofer whose assistant he had become. He had decided against the Professor and for Hitler who offered him fame and fortune as his loyal follower.

Hess Rises in the Nazi Party

After Hitler's seizure of power, Hess on April 21, 1931, was appointed Deputy to the Führer and on December 1, Reich Minister without Portfolio. On February 4, 1938, he was made a member of the Secret Cabinet Council and on August 31, 1939, appointed to the Ministerial Council for the Defense of the Reich. In these capacities he fulfilled manifold functions relating to Party leadership and the approval of all legislation suggested by the different Reich Ministers. When Hitler established a Central Political Commission in the party, he made Hess its head. Most importantly, Hess also served as personal secretary to the Führer. In the Third Reich it was Hess who decreed what universities and schools should teach. He initiated the formation of the German Labor Front. He regularly administered the oath of allegiance at Party rallies. An early enemy of the Jews, he greatly influenced the anti-Jewish legislation of 1935.

Hess shared the fanatic Nazi belief in the corruption of the Jews, but denied later that he bore responsibility for the German mistreatment of them. But he also asserted that if he would have had jurisdiction, "he would have done everything to protect my people from these criminals and I would not have had a bad conscience about it." Another time he declared that Jews wanted to take revenge on him, "since he had tried to end the war early which the Jews had started with so much trouble." The British M.P. [member of Parliament] Alrey Neave, not unfriendly toward Hess, commented that his statements "read like the product of a very sick mind." Hess also made "absurd accusations" against the medical staff in Nuremberg and Spandau that cared for him.

Mission of Peace

[On May 10, 1941, Hess embarked on an unauthorized flight to Scotland to enlist the help of Scottish rulers to persuade Britain to surrender.] Hess capped his adventurous flight to Scotland with a ludicrous demand that [British prime minister] Winston Churchill resign. The British government, ignoring his appearance on English soil, had him moved to the Tower of London, where he remained until October 1945 when he was transferred to Nuremberg for trial. There Hess, a mere shadow of more glorious times, feigned insanity or amnesia and delivered an incoherent final speech to the

Court. Having prematurely aged, he proved a difficult, even cantankerous prisoner at Spandau, complaining endlessly about his fate and treatment. His I.Q., according to G.N. Gilbert, prison psychologist, was estimated at 120, the fourth lowest among the defendants.

At the Nuremberg trial Hess showed "complete indifference" to the proceedings, in contrast to his co-defendants who were nervous and fully aware that they were on trial for their lives. With his eyes closed and not using the earphones provided for translation, Hess wanted to demonstrate his refusal to recognize the Court. He was convinced that the death penalty would be the unavoidable final judgment for all co-defendants. But his behavior aroused the ire of other defendants who were ready to fight for their lives and for Germany's "honor." This led to [Hermann] Göring's accusation that Hess was "disgracing" his colleagues. At other times Göring had considered Hess "always mentally slightly unbalanced." Baldur von Schirach, too, thought that Hess was "quite unworthy of the rank" Hitler had bestowed upon him.

A Willing Participant

Hess concluded his last remarks at the Nuremberg trial thus: He had been permitted to work for many years of his life "under the greatest son Germany had brought forth in its thousand-year history." He would not want to erase this period from his existence. He had been a "loyal follower of my Führer. I do not regret anything." Rendering final judgment on the first of October, 1946, Lord Justice Lawrence called Hess "the top man in the Nazi Party" and listed his often-repeated support of Hitler's policy of vigorous armament. "While he admittedly advocated international economic cooperation between 1933 and 1937, none knew better than Hess how determined Hitler was to realize his ambitions," "how fanatical and violent a man he was." "A willing participant" in the German aggression against several European countries—Austria, Czechoslovakia, and Poland—a "wholehearted supporter of all German aggressive actions" who justified these actions, he blamed Britain and France for the outbreak of the war. He proposed laws discriminating against Poles and Jews. . . .

Until his flight to England he was "Hitler's closest personal confidant" and must have been informed of the Führer's aggressive plans and helped them along. Hess supported all of Germany's aggressive actions up to his flight to Scotland, as he freely admitted once in Britain. Justice Lawrence thought Hess might have suffered from loss of memory and "mental deterioration" during the Nuremberg trial, but discarded the notion that he was not completely sane when he committed the acts of which he was charged. B. Hutton, author of *Hess: The Man and His Mission*, often defending Hess, concluded that Hess thought the Nuremberg trial would not be renowned for objective justice, but that strict adherence to its charter "could bring peace on earth to all men."

The New Führer

As Lieutenant Colonel Eugene K. Bird, U.S. Commandant of the Spandau prison and author of *Prisoner #7, Rudolf Hess* reported, Hess, after the execution of eleven of his co-defendants in Nuremberg, was rather "strangely cheerful." Seized by apparent self-delusion and preparing himself for a rebirth of the Nazi regime, it was his hallucination that he would not only some day walk out from Spandau a free man, but that he was destined to be the new Führer. He would take, however, this great responsibility only after the restoration of a united Germany, the union of West and East Germany. Having escaped death by hanging at Nuremberg, he was certain that a "great mission" awaited him. "Tomorrow the sun will rise again," he wrote to his wife on July 5, 1947. He would secure, he dreamed, the full cooperation of the Allies as well as that of the German people. Blinded by a false historical parallel between Hitler's seizure of power in 1933 and the likelihood of an early Nazi revival after World War II and totally misjudging the mood of the Allies as well as that of the German people, he saw himself taking over the leadership of the German people, unfolding the swastika once again.

In "Bulletin One," which he himself wrote in prison, he promised that he would turn to "the mass of my nationalistic friends and Party members," even drawing up a list of promising neo-Nazi candidates for important government posts. They should be released by the Allies to help in the rebuilding of the new German state. Among these were Hermann Esser, a close associate of Hitler, Otto Dietrich, former Nazi Press Chief, former members of Hitler's cabinet such as Schwerin-Krosigk and Walter Funk, not to omit his former driver Lipert and several other prominent SS men. He would also ask the allies for a limousine for himself and for three cars for his entourage, all German cars to be sure. All district *Gauleiters* [distric leaders] and high officers of the NSDAP [Nazi Party] would have to report promptly to their offices. To "protect" Jews—how many had survived?—from the "rage" of the German population, Hess suggested that they voluntarily settle into protective camps. Having apparently no knowledge of the cremation of his Nuremberg co-defendants who had been hanged, he made written provisions for creating honor guards for the graves of the eleven "martyrs" and for Göring and [Heinrich] Himmler who had committed suicide to escape the hangman. Generals [Wilhelm] Keitel and [Alfred] Jodl should be buried with full honors and their medals placed in their caskets.

No wonder that in the judgment of his co-defendants at Nuremberg Hess was considered a "paranoid" character. The judges had him examined several times. They had found his presentation before the Court marked by "rambling" and his general behavior bizarre. Hess had refused visits by his wife until 1969. He still admired Hitler. . . . He had never repented; to the contrary, had never repudiated his past record and had testified in court: "Even if I could, I would not want to erase this Nazi period of time from my existence." In the words of the U.S. commandant at Spandau, E. Bird, Hess was, "still proud and arrogant." "Poised between guilt and arrogance," he had maintained his silence. It was easier to say: 'I cannot remember.' Baldur von Schirach judged him similarly: "Hess had 'a curtain to pull down on the past; it was an act of self-preservation, a way of preserving his sanity'—a judgment with which Hess partly concurred." When he died in 1987 rumors circulated first that he had hanged himself. The British authorities in Berlin denied this categorically. The Allies decided on razing the Spandau prison to prevent any neo-Nazi attempt to make it a shrine to Hess and National Socialism.

3

Profiles · in · History

Hitler's Devotees

Martin Bormann: The Deputy's Deputy

Jochen von Lang

Martin Bormann traveled up the Nazi hierarchy by working behind the scenes. Originally hired as a deputy to Hitler's deputy, Rudolf Hess, Bormann seized the opportunity to become closer to Hitler after Hess's self-appointed peace mission to Scotland failed in 1941. In this selection Jochen von Lang shows how Bormann used his petty-bourgeois character to his advantage to gain Hitler's confidence. As the Nazi Reich progressed through the years of World War II, Hitler increasingly relied on Bormann's efficiency both in personal and public matters, and he made Bormann his most trusted secretary. Bormann was at Hitler's side during his last days in the bunker below the Reich Chancellery, issuing commands, sending communiqués, even helping Hitler write his last will and testament. For many years after the war, Bormann was thought to be alive and in hiding; now it is believed that he committed suicide as he tried to escape from Berlin shortly before the Russians took over the city. Lang, an editor for a German news magazine who wrote extensively about Hitler and the Third Reich, espouses this theory.

Jochen von Lang, "Martin Bormann: Hitler's Secretary," *The Nazi Elite*, edited by Ronald Smelser and Rainer Zitelmann, translated by Mary Fischer. New York: New York University Press, 1993.

❧ ❧ ❧

At the end of October 1945, as they lay rotting and starving in the rubble of their cities, with no hope for the future, the Germans heard that twenty-four of the most important men in the Third Reich were being prosecuted as criminals. The names were all familiar to them, except one: Martin Bormann. Now for the first time they learned of his many functions: National Director of the NSDAP [National Socialist German Workers' Party], General of the SS [Schutzstaffel, or protection troops], Chief of the Party Chancellery, Secretary to the Führer, and still more besides. In the indictment of the International Military Tribunal at Nuremberg he was accused of having contributed to the 'Nazi conspirators' seizure of power' before 1933 and thereafter of having taken part in a conspiracy against peace, the Geneva Convention and humanity.

This indictment was as vague as the whereabouts of the man himself; he was the only accused for whom the victors were still looking. They did not find him, in spite of 200,000 copies of a 'wanted' circular, newspaper appeals and radio announcements. He had always worked in the background and now he had melted away into it. The Allies had no idea of what they were losing in the process: as perfect a National Socialist as Hitler himself could have asked for. Because of this he had become Hitler's shadow over the years; in many respects he even became a man who directed the dictator, by deciding what his Führer was allowed to know. Hitler, who barely trusted anyone, trusted him almost unreservedly, and with good reason. From Hitler's point of view Bormann was his most loyal follower—to the very end.

The Ideal Official

To all external appearances Hitler's pre-eminent functionary was totally unremarkable, the average German
in every respect: 170 cm tall, dark eyes and prematurely
greying dark hair, a round head, bull necked, he had become overweight from attending banquets and drinking. He was as good at taking as at giving orders and he
carried them out without scruples. If he gave an order
there was no mistaking it; anyone slow on the uptake
might be helped on his way with a kick. He understood
quickly and immediately grasped essentials. Both at
work and at home he ruled absolutely. If a woman took
his fancy he made no attempt to restrain himself and
had taught his wife that she had to accept his affairs with
a good grace. In a party which reserved all the important
decisions for men this behaviour caused no offence.

His origins and Wilhelmine [taking after Kaiser
Wilhelm] ideals predestined Bormann to be the ideal
official. Although the son of a National Socialist petty
bourgeois [lower middle-class] family, he boasted of
coming from a Prussian military dynasty. In fact, his father was a post office clerk and had only been a trum-
peter for a time in a Hussar [Hungarian cavalry] regiment. His year of birth in 1900 should have singled out
Martin Bormann as one of those heroic youths who
overran enemy positions in the last year of [World War
I]. In fact, until his demobilisation he was batman to an
officer in the Naumberg garrison. The profession he
then studied was farming. He worked first as a trainee
on a big estate in Mecklenburg and then as a farm manager; he was however never a real farmer, who according to Nazi dogma would be the life source of the nation. He was director of two large concerns in the
Third Reich, but the only work he did there was with
his index finger.

Even as a young man he said he wanted to sooth the

sufferings of his vanquished people. In fact, he was convicted of having misdirected rationed foodstuffs. He
made a more ominous contribution to German revival
when he joined a North German *völkisch* (populist eth-
nic) league, became a member of an 'Association against
the Arrogance of the Jews' [in the words of Bormann],
and from his farm manager's desk he administered
hordes of shadowy figures whom the estates had given
lodging. They were demobilised soldiers who had been
unable or unwilling to gain a foothold in civilian life,
who as Volunteer Units defended the exposed eastern
border against Polish irregulars, and who were toler-
ated or even secretly supported by the governments of
the Reich as a counterweight against communist revolutionary schemes. Years later Martin Bormann wrote
in an NSDAP questionnaire that he had been 'sectional
leader of the Rossbach Organisation in Mecklenburg'.
This was a mark of honour in the NSDAP, for in its
early days it was a rallying point for this kind of super-
patriot. Bormann even said he went to prison with
some Rossbach members for 'love of the Fatherland.'
. . . The thanks of the Fatherland caught up with him
ten years later in the shape of a gleaming silver medal:
the Blood Order of the NSDAP.

According to Hitler's wishes, this decoration, to be
worn on a red ribbon, was originally to be given only to
those who had taken part in the attempted putsch of 8
and 9 November 1923. However after the invasion of
Austria anyone was allowed to adorn themselves with it
if they had been deprived of their freedom for at least
one year in the service of the swastika. When Bormann's Party Office devised this condition in 1938 he
too availed himself of this honour. He never wore other
decorations, although, like all of Hitler's constant companions, protocol allowed him to wear all sorts of exotic
insignia during state visits. . . .

Bormann: Party Assistant

Bormann went to Weimar, because his mother was well placed there, and since Captain Ernst Röhm's *Front-bann* was particularly active there, he joined it. By July of the following year, 1926, at the National Convention of the newly-established NSDAP in Weimar, he could already be seen standing in his brown shirt uniform alongside Hitler's big Mercedes, in which, as was to become the custom, the Führer saluted his followers' march past.

Six months later the Party became Bormann's employer—and remained so until the end. In Weimar he became the general factotum [assistant] for the Party District Executive: in exchange for pocket money he helped keep alive a struggling weekly newsheet by being its advertiser, representative, accountant, cashier and driver, because he had succeeded in buying himself a small car. He also drove speakers out to the villages. His first and last attempt to win supporters in a busy pub ended in stuttering and ultimately silence after ten minutes which he had laboriously managed to fill with the party's propaganda slogans. From then on he knew that he would get to the top in this party of fire-eaters, orators, saviours of the world and fighting cocks only if he developed his own strengths: assiduousness, the ability to settle complex matters quickly, to organise, to be a bureaucrat. Fanatical brutality towards opponents, ruthlessness with friends and devoted obedience towards those in command soon marked him out as suited for greater tasks.

When the director of a Nazi relief fund in the SA [Sturmabteilung, or storm troopers] High Command in Munich did not give the contributions to wounded fellow activists but put them in his own pocket instead, Bormann was given his job. In an amazingly short time he became an expert on insurance schemes. He . . . collected the contributions of all Party members in one special fund and paid out for loss or injury at his own discretion and without allowing recourse to law. When the Party could yet again not balance its accounts for propaganda material, a loan from Bormann's reserves made them solvent once more.

He also made sure of his career in other ways. He married Gerda Buch, the daughter of a former major and Party member from the earliest days of the NSDAP whom Hitler had nominated as Chief Justice of the Party. At the wedding nearly all the men wore brown shirts, including the Party boss, who came to the celebration to act as witness and put his car, the big Mercedes, at their disposal. Rudolf Hess, at that time (1929) the Fürer's secretary, had also come to the celebration. . . .

A Tool for Hitler

With the seizure of power in 1933, the Party mushroomed in size. This . . . prompted Hitler to restructure the Party hierarchy. Rudolf Hess, a political fool and therefore no rival, was now allowed to serve the Party as Hitler's deputy, but it was probably thought advisable to allocate him a Chief of Staff with a practical understanding of human nature, with burning ambition and unshakeable loyalty to the Führer: Bormann. As one who prided himself on his modesty, Hess had no need to fear that his new colleague could steal even a fraction of the glory of his new duties; Bormann stayed in the background. For this too he was rewarded; when Hess became even more demonstratively modest by dispensing with any mark of rank on his brown shirt—this was moreover just what the Führer had done—Bormann received the title of National Director of the Party and naturally along with it the tab with the golden eagle on a red ground on his brown jacket. . . .

[Bormann announced] in Hitler's name, naturally—

that the affairs of the Party could only be brought before their very busy Führer if they had first been
brought to the attention of his deputy (or of *his* deputy,
Bormann). Hess the dreamer naturally did not want to
be concerned with trivia; he liked to float above the
clouds—and not just as an aircraft pilot. Hitler therefore preferred to collaborate with Hess's Chief of Staff.
Bormann presented him with short documents which
lent themselves to swift decisions, had been evaluated
for their implications for Party policy and were legally
watertight—thanks to the steadily growing band of assistants in his steadily growing department.

Hitler had given assurances to people in Munich that
the Party National Directorate would stay in Munich.
Hess therefore felt obliged to stay there. Bormann
however gradually moved to Berlin where he was allowed to set up a small office in the Reich Chancellery.
Later a larger office was added close by, so that he had
all the documentation at hand when the Führer needed
something. Bormann soon had a regular place at
Hitler's lunch table. There his devotion occasionally
compelled him to take a meal from Hitler's vegetarian
menu, in spite of his own preference for juicy steaks,
and then he could not refrain from assuring those at the
table how much he was enjoying it.

He admired the Boss,—as Hitler was called in the
small circle of those constantly with him—honestly and
unreservedly, far more than most national or Party
comrades. Overpowered by his charisma and confirmed in this feeling by the successes of the first years
of government, he and countless other Germans transferred to their Führer one of the tenets of religious
faith: whatever he does is good, even if we fail to recog-
nise it at first. However Bormann had yet another reason for toasting himself in the glow of Hitler's favour;
his unexpected rise in the Party and the nature of his

duties constantly increased the number of his enemies and those jealous of him, and any who realised that Bormann himself was not to blame were offended by his brutal manner and the inconsiderateness of his methods. These too met with the Führer's approval. When he once happened to hear Bormann shouting at a colleague over the phone a grin spread across Hitler's face and he exclaimed 'That's letting him have it!' Many months later however he fended off complaints about Bormann, explaining that he needed this ruthless follower to win the war.

This comment reveals that even this constantly loyal follower, who was always ready for duty, was never more than a tool for Hitler, to be used as long as he needed it, and which he would have regarded as so much scrap when he no longer had any use for it. If Bormann had ever hoped that in time the Führer would treat him with more than goodwill embellished with a sprinkling of carefully calculated marks of distinction, for all his efforts he never gained anything more than a benevolent patron. . . .

The Deputy's Deputy

Because of Bormann's blind devotion Hitler regarded him as suited to organising private matters as well. The Führer concealed these almost more carefully than his state secrets; evidently he feared that he would lose the aura of being superhuman if he showed all-too-human traits. He left the administration of his fortune to the financial administrator who had proven his worth with the Relief Fund; given his artistic temperament he never bothered about financial matters. In this case his lack of respect for Mammon [material wealth] paid dividends: because the financial director collected whenever there was anything to be had. He also administered the millions from an 'Adolf Hitler Fund' from big business—honestly, but not entirely selflessly, since it increased his influence if he could give a hand to the leading lights of the Party after the expense of attaining new offices had led them into difficulties. . . .

Bormann displayed particular vigilance towards those who were in his opinion the most dangerous enemies of the Germans: Jews and priests. Party policy committed him to the persecution of the Jews in any case; a convinced National Socialist could do nothing wrong in that respect. The battle against the authority of the church and its servants was however more difficult; they sheltered behind the 'positive Christianity' which the Party had promised to protect. So Bormann had to confine himself to trimming back the traditional rights of the churches, such as religious education in the schools. He had protestant clerics, who had once supposed National Socialism to be an enemy of atheism, driven out of the Party. He promoted groups who depicted Jesus as a Jew

Nazi Party leader Martin Bormann, seen here to the right of Adolf Hitler, rose to become one of Hitler's closest and most influential advisers.

and overthrew his teaching. He banned everything Christian from his own family. His wife Gerda was instructed to protect the children from church influences at school or from playmates. Among the *Gauleiter* [district leaders] were some who disapproved of such a rigorous attitude. Most of them had gathered together their supporters themselves in the early days and only felt obliged to obey Hitler. With the agreement of the latter, Bormann intended to teach them to be more biddable. To this end each had a District Chief of Staff introduced into his office, a new functionary responsible to Bormann. They were no longer allowed to meet as a group without Bormann's permission. Their prerogative of free access to the Commander-in-Chief was restricted; they were now only allowed to invite themselves to lunch but they were not allowed to bring up matters pertaining to their duties there. Anyone who made himself unpopular went in fear for his office and prerogatives. . . . In Bormann's office lists were compiled of functionaries held in reserve to replace disobedient *Gauleiters*. Anyone who wanted to gain promotion in Party or state needed the approval of Bormann's chancery.

At Hitler's Side

No-one was better informed about Hitler's plans than he was. He was in Prague when the remnants of Czechoslovakia were made into a Protectorate. He was Hitler's shadow at the launch of a new battleship, a tour of inspection of the West Wall and at SS battle manoeuvres. He helped prepare for war. At the end of July 1939 Bormann was honoured when, in his family home in Pullach, Hitler informed a few selected members of the Party that within a few days he would change from being a rabid anti-Bolshevik into Stalin's accomplice. When the SS Personnel Office enquired of Bormann whether he already had a position, should war break out, he answered 'Not necessary, since if mobilisation occurs I will be at Hitler's side'.

On the evening of 3 September 1939, therefore, he boarded Hitler's special train, the first Headquarters. He had dressed up in field grey in an SS General's uniform, and in it he played at soldiers until the closing minutes of his life. However he never shot at the enemy, fighting instead on the 'home front' against defeatists, parasites, hangers-on, Christians and Jews. The Führer's military entourage were miserly in their respect of his Party office, but since he clung doggedly at Hitler's heels and could only be excluded from military briefings, he scarcely missed a single tip-off. He took care of important matters immediately, other paperwork ended up in a card index which he could refer to [at] some future date. If Hitler happened to be busy at Headquarters as Commander-in-Chief, then for all practical purposes Bormann was the first and last authority in civilian matters. If the Boss retired to the Berghof [Hitler's home in the Bavarian Alps], even generals had to stay down below on the plains. Party leaders were categorically only allowed to come when Bormann invited them, and he was a witness to nearly every conversation. Even [Hermann] Goering, [Paul Joseph] Goebbels and [Heinrich] Himmler had to accommodate themselves to his omnipresence. At Hitler's nightly monologues he was usually the only Party grandee among the listeners. It was typical that Hitler's initial, spontaneous reaction was to call Bormann when he was told that Hess had flown to Britain.

Two days later, on 12 May 1941, Hess's deputy to all intents and purposes moved into his former patron's place. As the director of the Party Chancellery he followed his Supreme Commander into the 'Wolfsschanze', set deep in the forest, where Hitler reduced his team of advisers to a 'Committee of Three': [Wilhelm] Keitel,

[Hans Heinrich] Lammers [Chief of Reich Chancellery] and Bormann, whose influence soon far exceeded that of his two colleagues. In April 1943 he fell heir to yet another title which Hess had held from the early days of the NSDAP: Secretary to the Führer; it allowed him to take part in every decision. Bormann intervened in the matter of exploiting the occupied lands to the east, in the decision to allow Polish children no more than a rudimentary schooling, and when the fate of shot-down enemy pilots was being discussed. When Goebbels proclaimed 'total war' to be the means of rescue from defeat after the catastrophe of Stalingrad, Bormann flung himself energetically into the plan and succeeded in playing a leading role in the 'levée en masse' [recruiting of able-bodied men for military service].

"We Trust Our Destiny"

After the attempt on Hitler's life on 20 July 1944 the Führer trusted almost him alone. The Army had committed high treason. The Air Force and its Commander-in-Chief had lied to him and failed. Ministers were unwilling to break laws as ruthlessly as their Führer demanded of them. The Waffen SS [German Army] was no longer providing the expected victories, the Gestapo was not capturing the enemies of the state in time and even the leader of the SS [Himmler], who always carried the oath of loyalty about with him on his belt buckle, was no longer free of suspicion of cultivating links with enemies within and without. Since the massacre of June 1934 [the Night of Long Knives, when Hitler had large numbers of SA liquidated] the SA had sunk to the level of a rifle club. And Germany's Allies? They had appeared after victories; now after defeats they were disappearing, one after the other. Even the Duce of Italy [dictator Benito Mussolini], once an admired model, was now a dictator without land or people. Enemy forces were advancing towards the German borders from the east, west and south and their aeroplanes were destroying the Reich almost unopposed. That might have made many a follower waver, but Bormann remained reliable and willing.

When reason had long since declared the war lost Bormann still, in spite of his understanding of the true situation, believed in Hitler's luck, in his supposed genius and even in miracle weapons. An imagined providence could not, in his belief, permit six years of privation, distress, fear, sacrifices of health and life to remain unrewarded. Bormann and his wife often encouraged each other to this effect in their letters. They sought prophetic consolation in historical novels and, like their Führer, after military defeats they kept up their spirits by remembering events from the reign of King Frederick II of Prussia.

On 5 February 1945 he wrote to Gerda from the destroyed Reich Chancellery: 'You would have to be quite an optimist to say we still had a chance. But we are. We trust our destiny. It is quite simply inconceivable that fate would lead our people and its leader along this wonderful path, for us finally to stumble and disappear'. For this staunch Party member there could be no defeat which would precipitate the nation into a super-Versailles [the treaty that ended Word War I] and which would confront him himself with the many crimes he had committed or simply condoned.

Finally he only had heroic rhetoric left with which to strengthen his resolve. On 2 April he wrote to his wife 'We will do our sworn duty to the end; and if we perish, . . . let us go proudly and unbowed!' He knew of course that nothing else could be gained by bowing. All he too had left was hope in the miracle on which Hitler the gambler was still speculating.

Faithful Bormann

The more the Reich dwindled, during the last few weeks of the war, into the Reichs Chancellery and the bunker underneath it, the closer Hitler and Bormann must have felt to each other. He was allowed to write down the latter's will and send it by courier to the Obersalzberg [one of Hitler's homes]. He could assign a few troops to each of his fanatical Party officials and send these small forces to strengthen morale in areas near the front—as executioners for defeatists. He instructed members of the Hitler Youth (boys and girls) to allow the enemy to sweep past them and then to commit acts of sabotage as Werewolves. His activism did not slacken as long as he still had the tools of his trade at his disposal: batteries of teleprinters, through which he sent commands, proclamations, entreaties and abuse almost without pause into the world above. Just as his Führer could only call upon shattered divisions for his 'blow for freedom', so Bormann's messages were at the end transmitted into a void. The ministers, *Gauleiter*, National Party Leaders, even Albert Speer, Heinrich Himmler and Hermann Goering were now only concerned with saving their own skins—from the enemy and from him too.

The faithful Bormann stayed in his Führer's underworld until the latter's body was half consumed in the flames. It is open to doubt whether he was sustained at this time by his ardent heroism alone. Tradition has it that, along with two generals he was friendly with, he drew courage from the cognac which was available in abundance—top quality French produce, of course. At the same time, in the last days of his life he had the satisfaction of being, along with Hitler, who had lost interest, the unrestricted ruler of the Reich. Of course it now measured only a few square kilometres.

In the night of 1 to 2 May 1945 the inhabitants of the

bunker attempted to break through the encircling Red Army. During this time Bormann disappeared. He wanted to take Hitler's political testament to Flensburg to Admiral Karl Dönitz and take up his office there at the same time. Hitler had nominated Dönitz as his successor and named Bormann as Party Minister. He never arrived in Flensburg. The Nuremberg judges would have been able to find Bormann's body if the Americans had believed the statements of the National Youth Leader, Artur Axmann. At the hearings he had stated that he had seen the Führer's Secretary dead at the first light of dawn, after the night he fled, in the vicinity of the Lehrter Station in Berlin. As it later transpired, Bormann had made use of the Nazi suicide pill, the capsule filled with prussic acid, which Hitler too had used. The corpse was buried as a nameless soldier not far from where it was found; after breaking out of the Führer's bunker Bormann had removed all marks of rank and all clues to his identity. Perhaps he would have had a chance of surviving unrecognised in prison. He had always remained a typical petty-bourgeois in every respect and was scarcely distinguishable from the millions who had trustingly followed Hitler.

Bormann was condemned to death in his absence on 1 October 1946 in Nuremberg, one of twelve accused. His skeleton lay undiscovered under the earth of the Exhibition Grounds in the Invalidenstrasse Berlin until 7 December 1972.

Albert Speer: Architect and Arms Minister

John K. Lattimer

In many ways, Albert Speer was an unlikely Nazi. He was shy, reserved, and polite. A failed architect, Hitler found in Speer the representation of all that he had one day hoped to be. As Hitler's minister of armaments, Speer directed the production of war matériel using slave labor. Tried at Nuremberg, Speer received a twenty-year sentence, which he served at Spandau prison. In the following excerpt from *Hitler and the Nazi Leaders: A Unique Insight into Evil*, John K. Lattimer portrays Speer as an intelligent man who came to the conclusion that Hitler was destroying Germany and attempted to take Hitler's life in order to bring an end to the destruction. Lattimer also feels Speer's knowledge of architecture could have played a great role in rebuilding the German infrastructure devastated by Allied bombing. Lattimer's positive portrayal of Speer shows why Speer was often referred to as "the Good Nazi."

Lattimer is a surgeon who served in the U.S. Army during World War II and who became chief of surgery at the Ninety-eighth U.S. Army General Hospital in Munich. After the war, Lattimer served as physician to the Nazi war criminals held in Nuremberg. *Hitler and the Nazi Leaders: A Unique Insight into Evil* contains his memories of the

John K. Lattimer, *Hitler and the Nazi Leaders: A Unique Insight into Evil*. New York: Hippocrene Publishing, 1999. Copyright © 1999 by John K. Lattimer. All rights reserved. Reproduced by permission.

prisoners. His other books include *Hitler's Fatal Sickness and Other Secrets of the Nazi Leaders: Why Hitler "Threw Victory Away."*

❧ ❧ ❧

Albert Speer was the other very impressive person among our prisoners [awaiting trial at Nuremberg] (along with [Hermann] Göring). He was certainly the most attractive of the group, and proved to be an extremely capable person. He was from a pleasant, upper-middle-class family, was well educated and very intelligent in a pragmatic way. His manner was quiet, boyish, almost shy, and he got along well with everybody, complying with all of the onerous regulations without difficulty and with unfailing politeness. Speer was fluent in several languages and often assisted the court interpreters when they stumbled over a word while trying to keep up with the difficult technical testimony. . . . He never objected to the sometimes overly restrictive actions of a new guard. The contrast between him and the rest of the loudly-complaining Nazis was noticeable.

An Efficient Nazi

I was astonished to learn that he was not only Hitler's personal architect, designing the monumental buildings that Hitler favored, but he had also been gradually placed in charge of *all* war production by the time the war ended. He had proved to be amazingly skillful as a manager when placed in total charge, and had greatly increased the production of arms, munitions, tanks, aviation gasoline, and finally, all warplanes. Freed from the conflicts of interest between competing departments, he doubled the production of fighter planes overnight and then kept the numbers increasing, even though the Allies bombed his factories every few days. He was a large-scale planner and an organizer of enormous ability, an example of the most competent type of German engineering mind, able to plan on a grand scale and to revise in order to execute the monumental job of war production. He was highly intelligent, belying the modest IQ score of 128 assigned to him by the modified type of routine psychological testing done by [Nuremberg's psychologist] Dr. [Gustav] Gilbert. There was a rumor that he had deliberately sought to "spoof" the intelligence tests, resulting in a score that did not truly represent his high degree of capability.

Speer had been by far the most productive of any of the men being tried, and was quite obviously better than any of the other German industrialists in the same work. He had benefited, of course, by inheriting the established organization of his predecessor Professor [Fritz] Todt, who very skillfully had built the autobahns, the "West Wall" forts, and the submarine pens, but who was killed in an airplane crash in 1942, thus elevating Speer to his position at once. . . . Psychologically, he was well-balanced and did not appear to be upset by anything that happened at the trial, ominous though things appeared at times. Speer said he had been attracted to Hitler, as were all the Germans, because of Hitler's potential to become a dynamic leader of a disorganized Germany. Hitler had discovered Speer, accidentally, through a good piece of work he had done in designing a building for the early Nazi Party. His cost overruns were far too high for the Party leaders, who fired him. Then Hitler discovered his grand designs. Hitler promptly "adopted" him and had him design numerous monumental buildings and memorials. From then on, cost was no problem.

Speer's ability to plan, design, and build on a grand

scale was exactly what Hitler wanted, since he repeatedly stated that a man is remembered only by the monuments he leaves behind. It was Hitler's declared intention to leave grand monuments to his memory, and Speer was exactly the person to help him do it. As it turned out, the only really great monument that was ever finished was the enormous Zeppelin Stadium in Nuremberg. Encompassing an area equal to several football fields, it has a colonnade of the most beautiful Italian marble along one side, about one quarter-mile long. Speer had been given the job of designing the German Pavilion for a World's Fair in Paris and made it outstanding by using searchlights to illuminate the tall structure as it soared into the sky. This gave it an ethereal quality that impressed everyone, including Speer. He therefore went on to augment the Nuremberg Zeppelin Stadium by surrounding the entire periphery with 150 military antiaircraft searchlights, each pointing straight up, for the great nighttime Party rallies. This created an enormous colonnade of light around the structure, which was most impressive. Later Speer reflected that his greatest accomplishments had not had too much substance, but were largely made up of light.

Speer admitted that he had been flattered by Hitler's attentions and enjoyed the unlimited access to methods, materials, and fine automobiles that his position carried. He was allowed to build for himself a beautiful little house, in the well-protected compound at Berchtesgaden. It resembled a modernized Japanese pagoda more than anything else. . . . It was around a corner and out of sight, so that the rest of the Nazi buildings (including Hitler's house) were not visible from it. He commented that Hitler was very kind to him and would never be rude or overbearing with him or the other architects. This was quite in contrast to Hitler's brutal demeanor with the politicians. . . .

Personal Responsibility and "Collective Guilt"

As the war continued, Speer gradually began to realize that Hitler was a tyrant and was destroying the country. He tried to reason with him but to no avail. He finally joined (though privately) in the thinking that Hitler had to be killed, but was frustrated in his plans to do so. In his testimony at the trial in a persuasive, straightforward, honest manner, he confessed his shock and repugnance at discovering the atrocities of the Nazi regime and recanted his attachment to Hitler and the Nazi government. Everyone who heard him, believed him, and there was a feeling among practically all of us who heard him speak that he would have been acquitted had it not been for one thing.

Running the country's wartime economy on the tremendous scale that he did, demanded some fourteen million laborers for Speer's work. One source for this labor force was the concentration camps. Speer maintained, and could prove, that he consistently asked for German civilian laborers and did not want displaced persons or concentration camp laborers, because the Germans were so much better as workers. He admitted, however, that he sometimes had to accept whatever was offered to him. These included a small number of displaced people and a very small number of concentration camp victims. During the trial, a damaging photograph was introduced, showing him visiting one of the concentration camps with [Austrian] Gauleiter [August] Eingruber. The prosecution insisted that they must have been talking about the use of inmates from that camp for his labor battalions. It was his only visit to such a camp and he was given the VIP tour of the good sections only. Speer could easily have denied that they were discussing laborers, but he made no effort to suggest that this was not the subject of their conversation. Against this background, he was sentenced to 20 years of imprisonment. . . .

He was inclined to self-flagellation at that point, and permitted the discussion to be led in such a way that it sounded as if he were soliciting more concentration-camp labor. We all listened to the slippery diplomats von Papen and [Minister of Economics Hjalmar] Schacht, manipulate the language to avoid negative implications and were amazed when Speer refused to do the same thing.

In his memoirs, Speer admitted that when he saw both [chancellor or Germany (1932–1933) Franz] von Papen and Schacht go free, he realized that he could have done the same. It was the opinion of all of the personnel at the trial who listened to Speer that, in his idealism, he had condemned himself in a way that was not entirely justified, certainly by comparison with the others. His own attorney was very upset at Speer's insistence on accepting responsibility for things outside his own ministry, but he was adamant on the matter of "collective guilt" of the entire group. . . .

Cooperating with the Americans

At the end of the war, Speer cooperated with American strategic bombing committees in a very helpful way. He advised them on what to do to Japan to cripple its industry in the most efficacious way, based on his own experience with American precision bombing. For example, he said that if we had only returned a second time to bomb the ball-bearing factory at Schweinfurt, Germany, as we had done on August 17, 1943, the Nazi war machine would have ground to a halt. Unfortunately [the Americans] did not realize this, and the damage . . . caused was repairable. . . .

Martin Bormann [Hitler's secretary after Rudolf Hess] clung continually to Hitler's side and endeavored to force Speer (along with everyone else) out of any position of influence with Hitler. He got his first opportunity to eliminate Speer when Speer came down with phlebitis after a knee operation related to a ski injury. He then had two large blood clots break off and damage his lungs in January 1944, while convalescing from the operation. . . .

In the in-fighting among Bormann, [Heinrich] Himmler, and Göring, one of the techniques of the Third Reich to get rid of a powerful rival, was to declare

Albert Speer (left) visits Paris, France, with Adolf Hitler. Speer came to disagree with Hitler's plans for Germany and worked against him at the end of the war.

that person sick and then eliminate him, implying that his condition had worsened. Speer was sure that this strategy was being used against him, so he had telephones set up in his sick room and ran his organization from there.

Gephardt [his doctor] had operated on his leg and had it in a plaster cast for three weeks. When finally allowed to stand, Speer had a violent pain in his chest and back and spat up blood. This was obviously from a pulmonary embolism (a blood clot to the lung). Gephardt purposefully ignored this and *again* got Speer up. Two days later, Speer had a second pulmonary embolism and nearly died.

Speer's wife then went to Dr. Karl Brandt, Hitler's doctor, who immediately sent Dr. Friedrich Koch, an internist at Berlin University, to examine Speer. Dr. Brandt specifically ordered Dr. Koch to be the *only* one in charge of Speer, and Koch stayed in a room near him night and day until he was better. It came out that Gephardt, Himmler and Bormann had decided that Speer was dangerous and getting too powerful and would have to "disappear." If Speer had died from the embolism, it would have been a convenient way for Bormann and Himmler to get rid of him. . . .

Speer and Hitler at Odds

At this time Speer learned that the American Eighth and Fifteenth Air Forces were concentrating on bombing the German aircraft industry out of existence. Once again Speer's production skills brought him back into the limelight and into Hitler's favor. At this time Speer asked for total mobilization of all the labor in Germany, including women, but in spite of this, Hitler still held back. . . .

By September 1944, it had become even more obvious to Speer that the war was lost and there was no possible way to save it. Hitler again reminded him that defeatist talk could be seen as treason. Speer again tried to persuade Hitler that the war was lost, on the basis of the production of armaments being completely destroyed by the bombing. He began to beg Hitler not to order the destruction of the electrical, fuel, bridge, communications, and railroad facilities in Germany, so the populace would be able to take care of themselves after the war was over. Speer knew that there was a passage in *Mein Kampf* where Hitler, himself, had written that "The task of diplomacy is to ensure that a nation does not go heroically to its destruction and that failure to follow this concept must be called criminal neglect of duty."

Now that Speer realized that Hitler was mentally impaired and intent on the destruction of Germany, he resolved to kill him. He located the air intake to Hitler's bunker in the garden in Berlin and set about trying to procure a supply of poison gas of the type used in the concentration camps. By the time he was finally able to do this, he found that Hitler (who had been gassed in WWI) had anticipated an artillery gas attack by the Russians and had had the air intake extended to a much higher level and guarded by armed sentries. Speer then spent the last several months of the war trying to devise ways to stop Hitler's orders to destroy Germany's infrastructure. Time and again he risked his life to countermand orders. Finally he had an arrangement made where all orders for destruction would be given only by his organization. He implied to Hitler that he would destroy things when the right moment came, but he never did. He even sent out messages to stop any anticipated "Werewolf" [ruthless attacks often made by German partisans] activity as being counterproductive, in that it would enrage the occupying powers who would then be even harder on the surviving German populace. Speer was able to stop the navy from destroying the port facilities by this stratagem.

The Surrender and Trial

After the surrender on May 8, Speer joined the new German Führer, Admiral Dönitz (his old friend) in the British zone. The British turned him over to the Americans, who interrogated him first for several days in the castle of Glücksburg, near Flensburg, near where Dönitz had his headquarters on the ship *Patria*. This was about May 24. Speer was then flown to our center at Mondorf and afterward taken to meet with the bombing experts of the American Air Force at the Trianon Palace Hotel at Versailles, and at the small palace at Chesenay nearby. Ironically, Speer had stayed there while he designed the spectacular German pavilion for the Paris World's Fair in 1937. The Trianon was now [U.S. general Dwight D.] Eisenhower's headquarters.

Speer contributed huge amounts of information about the success of various types of bombings and advised the Americans on how to attack the Japanese economy in the most effective way. At the end of this relaxed interlude, Speer was moved to Kransberg Castle (which Speer had rebuilt) for a few more days of interrogation and then, via another prison, to Nuremberg in late September.

The trial began with a devastating grand opening address by the chief American prosecutor Justice Robert H. Jackson. Speer took comfort from one sentence in which Jackson accused the defendants, but not the German people, of guilt for the regime's crimes. This thesis corresponded precisely with what Speer had hoped would be a subsidiary result of the trial, namely, that the hate directed against the German people, which had been fanned by the propaganda of the war years and had reached an extreme after the revelation of their crimes, would now be focused upon them, the defendants.

Dr. Gilbert was unfamiliar with Speer at the beginning of the trial and referred to him as the "Tall, shaggy-browed armaments minister, who attracted very little attention at first. He appeared to have a much more sincere and less demonstrative conception of the Nazi guilt than anyone else, however." He seemed to Gilbert to be the most realistic of all the prisoners; he told him that he had no illusions about his fate and that the indictments were no particular shock to him. He realized that history demanded such a trial in view of the enormity of the crimes committed, and considered it a good thing, in general. When Dr. Gilbert went from cell to cell asking each man to write a comment about his indictment, Speer quickly wrote, "The trials are necessary and is a shared responsibility for such horrible crimes, even in an authoritarian state." It was Gilbert's conclusion that Speer's repenting was not an expedient . . . but rather, he did indeed perceive that he had been on the wrong track in a disastrous way.

Speer pointed out that he had been made war production chief in 1942, without any previous experience. That he had told Hitler repeatedly that the war was lost and that they should save Germany from utter destruction, regardless of personal consequences. When Hitler had answered that if Germany couldn't win the war, it did not deserve to survive, it upset Speer greatly, shattering his illusions. It was then that he came to the conclusion that the whole Nazi system was rotten to the core and that he had made a terrible mistake in subscribing to Nazism and supporting Hitler as effectively as he had done.

Sincerely Guilty

It impressed everyone that Speer was much more sincere in his recanting of the crimes of the Nazi group. It was also notable that he did not try to evade the responsibility of his contribution to the war production effort. He agreed that he had something like fifteen million people in his organization, producing armaments of all sorts and that some of these people were from other countries and that a tiny number had indeed been concentration camp inmates. He repeatedly had to fend off the efforts of the SS to take over his production facilities for their own purposes, in order to improve their incomes. He had appealed to Hitler on various occasions to countermand the orders of Göring and Himmler, and whoever else was undermining his effort. He did this with outstanding success, getting Hitler to reverse himself several times in his favor. His rivals in the Nazi hierarchy repeatedly tried to do away with him, but failed, partly due to his very great competence and his sincerity in his work, all of which Hitler recognized and appreciated.

Speer recognized that in opposing the other members of the hierarchy, he was exposing not only himself but his family to assassination, but proceeded anyway. If it had not been for his efforts to preserve the bridges, the railroads, and the power plants of Germany from the destruction Hitler had ordered, the country would have been in a much worse state of chaos after the surrender.

It was clear to me that he was prepared to use his fantastic talents to help rebuild his shattered country. He knew where the few factories were that had been spared and how they operated and would have been a great asset to the rebuilding of the country. . . .

The court's final statement on Speer pointed out that he did not enter the Nazi government in a war capacity until 1942, so his indictments on charges one [conspiracy] and two [crimes against peace] were dismissed. However the evidence against Speer under counts three [war crimes] and four [crimes against humanity] related entirely to his participation in the slave-labor program. In mitigation, it must be recognized that he was one of the few men who had the courage to tell Hitler the war was lost and to take steps to prevent the senseless destruction of production facilities both in the occupied territories and in Germany. He carried out his opposition to Hitler's scorched earth program in some of the Western countries and in Germany by deliberately sabotaging it, at considerable personal risk. The fact that he had actively participated in plans to kill Hitler could have been a powerful argument in his favor, judging from the success of that ploy used by other defendants, but he did not pursue it.

In the end, Speer stoically accepted his sentence, looking the judge right in the eye, despite his realization that he might have done much better by very slight adjustments in what he said. It seemed to me that he made the mistake of talking too much, rather than just answering questions, as all good lawyers advise.

It occurred to many of us that his talents should have been put to work to alleviate the extreme hardship suffered by the German populace as a result of our devastating bombing. Thus his own tendency to self-punishment denied his people his services in the reconstruction period after the war. It was almost as if he demanded to be punished, and it got him 20 years in Spandau prison, so well described in his book, *Spandau Diary*. . . .

Speer admitted to being overcome by waves of depression at Nuremberg and at Spandau, but was able to control himself, and with his strong will, to come to terms with his situation. His depressions were short-lived and responded to exercise and absorption in drawing sketches of buildings. . . .

In the final analysis, Speer turned out to be by far the most likable and capable of the prisoners. He was always helpful, always amiable, and had shown tremendous capability as a manager of German war productions. . . .

After his release, Speer did well as an author and lecturer. He died quietly [in 1981] while on a trip to England, at age 76.

Ernst Röhm: SA Leader

Louis L. Snyder

Ernst Röhm was a bully who gloried in violence and cruelty; moreover, he believed that society wanted and needed such subversion and domination. It was just this character trait of Röhm's that attracted him to Adolf Hitler during the formative days of the Nazi Party. As leader of the SA (Sturmabteiling, the police force founded to protect Nazis), Röhm took part in the ill-fated 1923 Beer Hall Putsch. As the Nazi Party began to grow, however, Röhm's idea of national socialism favored socialism, whereas Hitler's favored nationalism, and a rift developed in the friendship between Röhm and Hitler. In the following excerpt from *The Nazi Elite: Shocking Profiles of the Reich's Most Notorious Henchmen*, Louis L. Snyder writes of Röhm's on-again, off-again relationship with Hitler. When Hitler heard that Röhm was threatening to use the SA to overthrow him, the Nazi leader had Röhm killed in a 1934 purge known as the Night of Long Knives.

Snyder, professor emeritus of history at the City University of New York and a student in Germany during Hitler's reign, has written nearly sixty books, most of them on Nazi Germany. His books include *The Nazi Elite: Biographical Sketches of Nazis Who Shaped the Third Reich*, *Encyclopedia of the Third Reich*, and *Hitler and Naziism*.

Louis L. Snyder, *The Nazi Elite: Shocking Profiles of the Reich's Most Notorious Henchmen*. New York: Hippocrene Books, 1989. Copyright © 1989 by Louis L. Snyder. All rights reserved. Reproduced by permission.

❧   ❧   ❧

Ernst Roehm [Röhm] was born in Munich on November 28, 1887, to an old Bavarian family of civil servants. Attracted at an early age by the military, he became a professional soldier and was commissioned just prior to the outbreak of World War I. In combat he became known among his comrades as a fanatical, simple-minded swashbuckler who delighted in showing off his contempt for danger. In terms of war service, he was a good soldier. He took joy in the camaraderie of war and became a battle casualty in the process. Although thrice wounded, he insisted on being returned to the front each time ready for more combat. Half his nose was shot away and there was a bullet hole in his cheek. He thereafter faced the world as a disgruntled veteran ready for trouble wherever he could find it.

A *Freikorps* Member

Like others who became leaders in the Nazi hierarchy, Roehm turned to the *Freikorps*, postwar freebooters who claimed they were working for the regeneration of Germany. The *Freikorps* became the training unit for those terrorists who played a significant role in German life in the immediate postwar years. Roehm also retained his post as captain in the *Reichswehr*, [armed resistance], Group Headquarters A, in Munich. At the same time, he was prepared to support the freebooters and their policy of evading limitations placed by the Treaty of Versailles on Germany's military strength. By backing the *Freikorps*, he saw the nucleus of a new army that would eventually avenge the humiliations forced on Germany by the postwar treaty.

The tough little freebooter was attracted by the great

arsenal left behind by the defeated German Army. These arms were supposed to be destroyed by order of the peace treaty. Captain Roehm was able to persuade the Allied Control Commission that old armored cars and rusty machine guns were of no use in serious warfare, but they could be used effectively to prevent the spread of Bolshevism to the West. It was an effective argument. . . .

At the same time, Roehm turned his attention to war on the political front. He was interested in any party that could capture the working classes for a nationalist and militarist cause. The German Workers' Party had all the qualifications. At this time, Hitler was building up his movement and he needed the support of such tough veterans as Roehm. The thick-necked captain and his followers were just the right men to fight Communists in the battle of the streets. Roehm persuaded his colleagues to join the Nazi ranks. From these units came Hitler's first strong-arm squads, later to emerge as the notorious Storm Troopers. . . .

Assisting Hitler

Meanwhile, a strong friendship developed between Hitler and Roehm. The two used the familiar "*Du*" ("thou") in conversation. From the beginning, Hitler was aware of Roehm's [homo-] sexual preference but he decided at the time to pay little attention to it. The man was too valuable. He was indispensable in obtaining the protection of the army as well as the Bavarian government. Throughout his early career the budding young politician needed the tolerance of the army for his own campaign of violence and intimidation. Moreover, Hitler felt that Roehm and his bully boys, who took pleasure in smashing skulls, were absolutely essential in the Nazi drive for power.

In August 1921 the Weimar government, under pressure from the Allies, ordered the dissolution of the *Freikorps* and other nationalist organizations. To keep his disbanded forces together Roehm organized a "Gymnastic and Sports Division" inside the Party. Its membership was the same as the freebooter units dedicated to winning the battle of the streets against the Communists. Later that year, in October, its name was changed to *Sturmabteilung* (the *SA*, or Storm Section). In December 1922 Hermann Goering, who had won a reputation as flying ace in World War I, was made commander of the brown-shirted Storm Troopers.

Hitler now had his private army and he was grateful to Roehm for its personnel and arms. The NSDAP, the National Socialist German Workers' Party, could muster a strong force to embody and propagate the military idea. The new *SA* was pledged to cultivate loyalty between comrades, and "joyful obedience to the Leader."

In late September 1923 Roehm decided to resign from the *Reichswehr*. His reasons were not altogether clear. It was rumored at the time that he was the target of government investigations about armament swindling. In any event, his role as a liaison between Hitler and the army was at an end. He chose now to turn all his efforts to supporting a National Socialist revolution under the leadership of Hitler.

The Beer-Hall *Putsch*

Roehm played a role in the bizarre Munich Beer-Hall *Putsch* of November 8–9, 1923. The entire idea brought him into a state of euphoria. This was the kind of action the swashbuckler craved. He appeared on the scene with a fully packed soldier's kit as if prepared for a week's stay in the trenches. There was something pitiful about this schoolboyish desire for action.

Together with a small band of followers, Roehm occupied army headquarters during the night of November 8, when Hitler was leading his dramatic coup at the Beer Hall, the *Bürgerbräu Keller*. At dawn Hitler returned to the hall, leaving Roehm to hold out at his assigned post.

Meanwhile, troops of the regular army surrounded Roehm and his men. Both sides were reluctant to open fire. Many lower echelon officers of the army sympathized with Roehm and his battle against the Treaty of Versailles. The trapped Nazis sat back to await events.

When the Munich police fired on the Nazi parade, leaving sixteen Nazis dead in the streets, the intended coup was smashed. Two hours later, Roehm was persuaded to capitulate at Army headquarters and was taken into custody. Roehm was one of the nine in addition to Hitler who were accused of treason. Although found guilty, Roehm was discharged on the day sentence was pronounced.

Building the *Kampfbund*

While Hitler was serving his sentence at Landsberg Prison, Roehm set about the task of rebuilding the movement. An able organizer, he began to reconstruct what he now called the *Kampfbund* (Militant League). He journeyed from one end of Germany to the other, proposing, arguing, demanding. He even went to Austria to bolster his rebuilding campaign. Within a short time, he had some thirty thousand men enrolled in his *Kampfbund*.

Meanwhile, Hitler in his cell at Landsberg was having some doubts about his swashbuckling friend. Above all, the *Fuehrer* wanted no powerful challenge to his own leadership. In common with gangsters everywhere and at any time, as top man he maintained a divide-and-rule policy which would have his henchmen at each other's throats. This was the instinctive Machiavellianism which he regarded as absolutely necessary for his cause.

The more successful Roehm was in his campaign of

reconstruction, the more uneasy Hitler became. The Bavarian government arrested several *Kampfbund* leaders and even delayed Hitler's parole because of their activities. Roehm later wrote that Hitler felt that his approaching release was endangered and laid the blame, not on the enemy, but on the friends who were fighting for him.

Moreover, Hitler was annoyed by Roehm's creation of the *Kampfbund* as successor to the *SA*. He was not pleased by Roehm's initiative. In his eyes the *SA* was designed merely as a political front for the Party and must always remain subordinate to it. Roehm disagreed. He saw his Storm Troopers as a military movement and made the demand that they be given appropriate representation in the parliamentary group "and that they should not be hindered in their special work."

It was a serious crack in the Nazi structure.

The issue came to a head in April 1924. In a meeting with Roehm on April 16, Hitler told Roehm bluntly that the *Kampfbund* must go and that the *SA* must be reconstructed from the ground up. He, the *Fuehrer*, would not accept Roehm's claim that the political and military movements were entirely independent of each other.

The next day an angered Roehm wrote to Hitler resigning from leadership of both *Kampfbund* and *SA*. "I take this opportunity, in memory of the great but difficult hours we have had together, to thank you for your comradeship. I urge you not to exclude me from your personal friendship."

There was no reply. When, on February 27, 1925, Hitler called a mass meeting at the Bürgerbräu Keller, Roehm was pointedly absent.

Leaving Germany

Craving action in the old style, Roehm went off to Bolivia to serve in its army. Like other German officers who were without work, he moved to South America to enjoy a steady income in a post for which he felt himself to be professionally qualified. He remained in Bolivia for more than five years.

In 1930 Hitler was having trouble with his revived Storm Trooper organization. Prior to the elections of September 1930, the Berlin *SA* mutinied and destroyed the Nazi Party's headquarters. Storm Troopers claimed that they were not getting the pay promised them. In addition, there was strong discontent with leadership. Hitler tried to correct the situation by levying a special tax on all Party members for the benefit of his Storm Troopers. In hectic meeting with the rank-and-file, he finally managed to bring his dissidents around by promising better pay and more effective leadership.

Even though his Party went on to electoral successes, Hitler did not forget his troubles with the *SA*. He got in touch with Roehm, urging him to forget the past and return to Germany to take over his post as Chief of Staff. He needed a tough-minded taskmaster who could keep the *SA* in hand. On his part, Roehm regarded his recall as fully justified. Had he not, along with Goering and Goebbels, been at Hitler's side during the two years before the Nazis took power? . . .

A Rift Develops

But a gap was widening between the two comrades. There were two issues at stake: Roehm's desire to incorporate his *SA* into the regular army, and his leaning toward a Second Revolution, the proposed socialist side of National Socialism. In both cases irreconcilable differences rose between the two former comrades-in-arms.

Hitler remained loyal to his compact with the generals. He told his *SA* chieftains that they formed "an army of political soldiers" who had won the German Revolution for him. True, they had defeated the Communists in the streets, but now that National Socialism had emerged victorious, the Party had no further use for them. He, Hitler, had to compromise with existing institutions, especially the *Wehrmacht*, and he intended to remain loyal to the "glorious old Army."

Angry repercussions from Roehm. His Brown Shirts had won the revolution for Hitler. They had committed excesses in the process, he admitted, but this was no time to cast aside the faithful troopers who had boosted Nazism to power. In a speech delivered in November 1933 before top officers of the *SA*, he bitterly attacked "reactionaries," businessmen, and army officers, all of whom Hitler now relied upon for help. The *SA*, he said, had not lost its reason for existence. If necessary, he would see to it that "these gentlemen will be changed in a gentle, or if necessary, an ungentle manner." His brawling street fighters knew exactly what he meant.

A National Socialist Struggle

Added to the army question was the considerably more important issue of the so-called Second Revolution. Since the early days of the Party, Roehm, along with Gregor Strasser and others, formed a left-wing branch that leaned toward the socialist side of the National Socialist movement. Hitler had won his way to power by emphasizing a nationalist ideology, by utilizing the help of the army, industrialists, and bureaucracy. Roehm and others began to call for an extension of the Party's socialist aims. "The National Socialist struggle," he said, "has been a Socialist revolution. It has been a revolution of the workers' movement. Those who made this revolution must speak for it." The implication was that the *SA* would see to it that the revolution would not slow down.

Dismaying dilemma for the *Fuehrer.* He wanted to retain Roehm as a good Party comrade, but he also needed the support of both army and industrialists. And those two interested parties had only contempt for Roehm and his aggregation of roughnecks and misfits. Hitler felt that he had no choice in the matter. The regular army refused to take in the Storm Troopers, and the financial interests were utterly opposed to the idea of a Second Revolution.

Trying to reason with Roehm, Hitler sent for him on June 4, 1934, and in a five-hour meeting literally begged his old comrade to conform. "Forget the idea of a Second Revolution. Believe in me. Don't cause any trouble." The *Fuehrer* promised that he would not disband the *SA*, to which he owed so much. But the matter was becoming critical. He ordered the Brown Shirts to go on leave for a month, during which time no uniforms were to be worn. Another meeting with Roehm was arranged for July 1 at Bad Wiessee.

The Night of Long Knives
The close friendship between Hitler and Roehm came to a tragic end during the Blood Purge of 1934, also called The Night of Long Knives. The *Fuehrer* decided to unleash an "educational campaign" against the growing power of the *SA*. In the process, seventy-seven leading Nazis were to lose their lives, including Ernst Roehm. There were, in addition, many other victims of the purge.

On the morning of June 29 Hitler, at the time staying at a hotel in Bad Godesberg overlooking the Rhine, summoned Viktor Lutze, *SA-Obergruppenfuehrer* (general) of Hanover and informed him that he was to succeed Roehm as *Stabschef* (Chief of Staff) of the *SA*. Astonished, Lutze accepted at once. Meanwhile, Goebbels flew in from Berlin to be at the *Fuehrer's* side. He told Hitler that Karl Ernst, *SA* chief in Berlin, was at that moment alerting Storm Troopers "certainly for some ill purpose." It was a calculated lie: Ernst, who had just been married, with Roehm and Goering in attendance, was on his way to Bremen with his bride and was about to board a passenger ship for a honeymoon in Madeira.

At one o'clock on the morning of June 30, Hitler received urgent messages from Goering and Himmler to the effect that an *SA* uprising was being synchronized in Berlin and Munich for the following day. Both Goering and Himmler knew that Hitler was supposed to meet his old comrade Roehm within the next few hours. Soon the entire *SA* was supposed to go on leave. The two plotters knew that few would believe the tale of a massive *SA* conspiracy.

Hitler was stirred into action. This was to be the Second Revolution and he would stifle it at its proposed birth. He made the drastic decision to purge the traitors. He ordered Goering to take care of the situation in Berlin, and that two companies of his personal *SS* bodyguard, under command of Sepp Dietrich, be sent from Berlin to Munich.

Hitler, accompanied by Goebbels and Lutze, flew from an airport near Bonn southward across Germany. His plane landed at Munich at 4 A.M. At the Ministry of the Interior two chiefs of the Bavarian *SA* saluted the *Fuehrer*, only to be greeted with an outburst of hysterical rage. Hitler tore off the insignia of rank from the shoulders of the astonished officers and screamed abuse at them. He drew his revolver, but before he could use it, one of his bodyguards shot the men at close range. Hitler kicked one of the corpses and remarked: "These men were not the most guilty."

Gathering together his *SS* guards, Hitler set off at the head of a cavalcade of cars for Bad Wiessee. His goal was to deal personally with Roehm, who was staying with several associates at a private hotel. Roehm lay in bed, fast asleep. . . .

Hitler raced toward Roehm's own room and banged loudly on the door.

"Who is there?" Roehm called sleepily.

"It is I, Hitler. Open up!"

Roehm unbolted the door, saying: "Already. I wasn't expecting you until tomorrow."

"Arrest him!" Hitler shouted to his aides.

Roehm stared dumbfounded at the open doorway crowded with Hitler's band. Together with other prisoners he was hustled into a car and taken at great speed to Munich.

Meanwhile, Goering and Himmler in Berlin went ahead with their part of the blood bath. Top *SA* leaders suspected of disloyalty to Hitler were arrested and placed in a coal cellar at the Lichterfelde Cadet School barracks. Most had no idea why they were being shot. Some went to their death shouting *"Heil Hitler!"* . . .

Hitler arrived at the prison to meet the sullen Roehm. Defiantly, Roehm demanded to see his friend, Adolf, the man he had launched on his career. Surely Adolf would understand his loyalty. But now Hitler wanted no meeting. Instead, he snapped a new order: "Shoot his chauffeur Max. And tell him what you have done. Lock him in his cell and await my orders."

Hitler then demanded that a revolver be left in Roehm's cell so that he could take the "honorable" way out.

Roehm refused to use it: "If I am to be killed, let Adolf do it himself."

On July 2, two *SS* officers, acting on the order of Sepp Dietrich, entered Roehm's cell. Stripped to the waist, Roehm was about to say something but he was told coldly to shut up. The *SS* men emptied their revolvers into him at point-blank range. With an expression of contempt on his face, Roehm slumped to the ground.

Joachim von Ribbentrop: Hitler's Diplomat

John K. Lattimer

Joachim von Ribbentrop was an aspiring actor who used dramatics to cut an impressive figure as a diplomat. A late-comer to the Nazi Party, Ribbentrop did not join until 1932. Ribbentrop used his sociable wife and her family's wealth and connections as part of the champagne-producing Henckel family to garner Hitler's favor. Hitler saw in Ribbentrop and his wife a means of reaching out to foreign countries, and he used their sphere of influence to further his own diplomatic causes. After World War II Ribbentrop was charged with war crimes and tried at Nuremberg. In prison he never wavered in his loyalty to Hitler and repeatedly professed his faithfulness. He was hanged as a war criminal on October 16, 1949. In this excerpt from his book *Hitler and the Nazi Leaders: A Unique Insight into Evil*, John K. Lattimer presents a comprehensive background on Ribbentrop. Lattimer describes Ribbentrop's work habits and the demands he imposed on staff and coworkers. The author shows how, in the last days of the Third Reich, Ribbentrop tried to arrange peace with the Western Allies.

Lattimer is a surgeon who served in the U.S. Army dur-

John K. Lattimer, *Hitler and the Nazi Leaders: A Unique Insight into Evil.* New York: Hippocrene Publishing, 1999. Copyright © 1999 by John K. Lattimer. All rights reserved. Reproduced by permission.

ing World War II and who became a physician to the Nazi war criminals held in Nuremberg. His other books include *Hitler's Fatal Sickness and Other Secrets of the Nazi Leaders: Why Hitler "Threw Victory Away."*

❦   ❦   ❦

Joachim von Ribbentrop was born in 1893 in the German Army garrison town of Wesel. His overbearing, army-officer father pressured him to excel. The family moved to Switzerland when he was ten years old.

Ribbentrop's formal education was carried only up to elementary school, whereupon he was sent to Grenoble in France to study languages at which he became quite adept. He was offered a chance to live with a family in England which delighted him; he learned English both in London and in Canada. In 1910, he was an aspiring actor, but his British accent was so exaggerated that even his fellow actors mocked him. Years later, his propensity to act out roles was quite apparent in his skill at making an entrance and in his apparently effortless and quite unique way of raising his arm when he said "Heil Hitler." His rivals were sure that this was the result of many hours of practicing before a mirror.

In Canada he worked as a bank clerk and for the railroads, in addition to acting. In New York he was a newspaper reporter. When World War I became imminent, he sailed for home, lest he be interned.

World War I Officer
In World War I, Ribbentrop served as an officer with modest distinction. He charmed his way into an exclusive cavalry regiment and was awarded the Iron Cross, First Class, The Order of the White Falcon, The Old-

enburg War Cross, and The Hamburg War Merit Cross. Toward the end of World War I, he . . . came down with active tuberculosis. He was hospitalized briefly, but after a short tour of duty in Turkey he stayed on as a lieutenant at the war ministry. He was there until 1919 when he met Anneliese Henckel of the champagne producing family, at a tennis tournament. (Ribbentrop was not only an excellent tennis player, he also played the violin well enough to be in several concerts. He was also a bobsled champion at Arosa, in the Swiss Alps.)

Anneliese was a wealthy, rebellious girl who was chic but not a real beauty. Moody, irritable, and prone to sinus headaches, she was well aware of her family's contempt for Hitler and her outspoken mother's contempt for Ribbentrop. His monocle and his "trick title" were particularly detested. Despite her family's objections to Ribbentrop, Anneliese married him in 1920 and he was taken into the firm, but only as a champagne salesman, never as a partner. His good tailoring and his fluency in French and English were great assets in this field, and his job took him to other countries. Ribbentrop prospered wonderfully in the international champagne business: it was not only profitable, but he quickly discovered that gifts of liquor were an entrée to politically powerful people. He used this approach liberally and skillfully at home and abroad, encouraged by Hitler.

Ribbentrop as Foreign Minister

The other Nazis were openly contemptuous in their remarks about him and were especially critical of his capability to be the foreign minister for their country, a job for which he had no real qualifications. The veteran diplomats, like [Konstantin] von Neurath whom Ribbentrop had displaced, were critical of one incident after another, such as when the nonaggression treaty had been proposed but von Neurath had refused to sign it. On this occasion, to please Hitler, Ribbentrop stepped right up and signed it, even though his post was only that of minister-at-large. Two years later, however, he was elevated by Hitler to the exalted position of foreign minister. [Economic Minister Hjalmar] Schacht, [Vice-Chancellor Franz] von Papen, and [Grand Admiral Karl] Dönitz were abundantly critical of practically everything he had done, but recognized that Hitler had used him to accomplish his goals: Ribbentrop acted as the front for maneuvers that Hitler knew he was going to repudiate very shortly, such as the Munich Pact. This was a travesty that Hitler intended to violate and quickly did. The 1939 nonaggression pact with Stalin and the Russians was also set up by Ribbentrop, under Hitler's direction.

Hitler was bored and uncomfortable with entertaining, and happy to have Ribbentrop entertain foreign dignitaries and please them with gifts of fine liquors. He therefore encouraged Ribbentrop's liquor business to grow, even during the war. Ribbentrop became wealthy enough that he could buy his way into positions of power in the diplomatic arena, without worrying about the expense. During his business trips abroad, he became cognizant of his ability to sell the German government's viewpoint. Ribbentrop had only joined the Nazi Party in 1932. He was first introduced to Hitler by [former German chancellor] Count [Bernard] von Bülow, as an interpreter of the French and British newspapers. Touted as a member of a wealthy, worldly family, he greatly pleased Hitler in this role. (It seemed obvious to [prison psychiatrist] Dr. [Douglas M.] Kelley that Hitler was a "father" figure in Ribbentrop's psyche and that Hitler had "played him" to the limit for his own purposes. Ribbentrop's egocentric displays were so repulsive that Dr. Kelley was sure they were a psychiatric manifestation of his insecurity. He completely fell apart in prison, acting like a child who had lost all his anchors to stability.)

Hitler was happy to have Ribbentrop join the movement in 1932. With von Papen now the Chancellor under [Paul von] Hindenburg, he used Ribbentrop to try to get himself named vice-chancellor but Hindenburg refused. Then, upon Hindenburg's death, Hitler not only became chancellor but declared himself Führer.

He was so impressed with Ribbentrop that he called on him for advice on foreign relations to a surprising extent. Very early, he gave him an office for his "Ribbentrop Bureau" across the street from the foreign office. He was asked to prepare a daily summary of foreign news from the newspapers. On this basis he became Hitler's foreign policy advisor, much to the annoyance of the diplomatic corps. He was then appointed to the foreign office in a minor official post, about 1934, but Hitler then amazed everyone by naming him ambassador to Great Britain in 1936.

Another big surprise to me was the very powerful role that Ribbentrop's wife played, not only in his life but in the gentrification of the entire Hitler inner circle. It was she who had urged Ribbentrop to expand his use of gifts of rare vintages to attract the attention of influential people in the new government. Frau Ribbentrop volunteered to give several, very dignified, small dinner parties for Hitler so he could entertain notables. Hitler loved the expensive furnishings, the well-run house, and the perfect servants. (Hitler referred to the Ribbentrops as his "upper-crust" representatives, even though the Ribbentrops were never really in the top drawer of Berlin society, according to Frau Ribbentrop's mother.) . . .

It seems undeniable that Anneliese's influence caused Ribbentrop to rise so rapidly in the diplomatic service. He had absolutely no qualifications or experience in the field, aside from knowing some champagne dealers (and their titled clients) in other countries, especially

England. It was his name-dropping to Hitler that gained him the ambassadorship. He and his wife cut handsome figures at official functions where they were seen with royalty.

A Family Man

Eventually Hitler recalled him to Germany and used him as a diplomat-at-large to negotiate treaties and agreements (that Hitler had no intention of honoring). Hitler came to realize that in Ribbentrop he had a follower who was completely devoted to him, and began to use him to the hilt. This is what led eventually to his being appointed foreign minister in 1938. It was said that Ribbentrop quickly learned [Reichsminister Hermann] Göring's trick of finding out Hitler's own views on any issue and then presenting them to him, as his own. Frau Ribbentrop was a tremendous help to Joachim in all ways. She was his tower of strength in all of his interactions. She realized she could mold his career into a grand success with Hitler. She also recognized Ribbentrop's weaknesses, revelling in the fact that he depended on her and was succeeding primarily as a result of her machinations. They were very devoted, appreciating each other's mutually valuable points.

They had five nice-looking children: two girls and three boys who always looked a little skeptical when they were summoned to have their picture taken with Hitler. There was no doubt that Frau Ribbentrop's mother recognized her son-in-law's weakness. She frequently made caustic remarks to her friends to the effect that of all her sons-in-law, the one that was the stupidest had risen to the greatest heights. Ribbentrop's wife's devotion was also manifested during the trial. When she was denied any opportunity to see him for over a year, she nevertheless came frequently to the prison, waiting patiently for any word or information about him. Frau

Ribbentrop also wrote books about her husband's career, publishing them privately, and kept up a brisk correspondence with anyone who wished to know more about him. She had persuaded him to negotiate for a noble title so he could use the word "von" before his name, and had designed a coat of arms which appeared on their stationery and silverware. . . .

A Diplomat with Theatrical Style

Göring, von Neurath, Schacht, and von Papen were scathing in their criticism of Ribbentrop and would quote one blunder after another that he had made. For example, when he was presented to the King of England as the incoming ambassador from Germany, he approached him and then put out his arm in the Nazi salute. This enraged the British who disliked him bitterly from then on. At a luncheon to introduce the new ambassador to London's upper crust, Ribbentrop launched into a Hitlerlike harangue for forty minutes. Winston Churchill, out of his sight, began to mimic him, to the great amusement of the audience. Frau Ribbentrop could see Churchill and was furious.

Because of his insecurity and the knowledge that the other members of Hitler's hierarchy were a hard-driving group of backstabbers, Ribbentrop surrounded himself with loyal "flaks." He became so arrogant and disdainful that it was difficult for anyone to approach him. . . . Even his employees pointed out that he would come into a room and act as if no one else were there, making an appearance of suddenly realizing their presence. After that, he treated them like dogs. One of their greatest complaints was that he would require his entire staff to line up at the airport and wait for hours until his plane arrived. If his wife was with him they would all have to bring their wives. Sometimes they would wait in a pouring rain for Ribbentrop to arrive, after which he would simply march off to his car, with a wave to the rain-soaked staff.

Everyone acknowledged his theatrical style: his uniforms and his gestures. He had special uniforms designed for his staff, adorned with medals. He even got Hitler to help him design them. Any official function was preceded by lengthy memorandums indicating how to attend to every tiny detail. Göring described him as a boundless egotist, a wine salesman who was successful in business but had neither the background nor the tact for diplomacy. Göring tried to advise Hitler to remove Ribbentrop for two reasons: First, Ribbentrop was hated by the British after his insulting introduction to the King; second, he also started advising them on how to compete with Russia, not realizing that the British considered themselves the experts in that area. They were actually trying to give the Germans advice about how to protect Germany from the Russians. . . .

A Devoted Nazi

According to his secretary, Ribbentrop was extremely demanding of his staff. Any order had to be executed immediately. He denied himself any extended private life, had a reckless disregard for his own health, and expected the same from his subordinates. He said that his work meant more to him than anything else, and he demanded a similar attitude from his staff. Whenever great things were in the making, his "drive" inspired everybody. Everybody happily did the jobs assigned to them. During that time, you couldn't tell if it was day or night, but when the job was finished, he always showed his appreciation. Even in normal times, however, his schedule was unusual. He was indeed a natural "night worker," apparently suffering from insomnia. He could not get to sleep before 3:00 A.M., so he seldom went to bed before 2:00 A.M. He did not like to awaken before 9:30 A.M. Presentations by his advisors started his day and often delayed midday dinner until three or four o'clock. Meal times were no relaxation either since he monopolized the conversation and discussed only his official and political matters. If one of his sons had just returned from a vacation, he might be asked to tell about it briefly, but this happened very seldom. Occasionally he would have a movie shown in the offices at night. He preferred pleasant, humorous films. This left him no time for reading or the cultivation of hobbies. He had a very good memory and could converse intelligently on many topics about which he had had no formal education. He loved to astound experts with bits and pieces of inside information.

He loved music, having been an excellent "concert" violinist as a youth. Before the war he had attended concerts and plays occasionally, but ceased doing so during the war. He preferred [composers Richard] Wagner and [Ludwig van] Beethoven. He was also interested in painting and in hunting. Any time he went on a hunting trip, however, he took the staff with him and everybody stood ready for work at any moment.

He had had no severe illnesses between the two world wars, until 1943, when he came down with pneumonia. This raised the specter of tuberculosis again, but it subsided with rest and a "sulfa" drug. He had his staff bring reports to his sickroom and he dictated and telephoned his instructions from his bed—even while he was still somewhat ill. Hitler demanded that he move his headquarters to East Prussia, and he did so at great risk, according to his doctors. He would follow his doctors' instructions for a few days but then gradually begin to get back to his routine of overwork. He ate, drank, and smoked very little. His secretary considered him to be an extremely clever man with complete idealistic devotion to his mission to improve the foreign policy of Germany. He had been an absolute outsider when he started in the foreign service and he had all the disadvantages of an amateur. His temper did not tolerate any obstructions or difficulties, which made things difficult for everybody.

An Efficient Organizer

Still, he completely reorganized the deteriorated foreign office, according to his secretary. She said he improved the existing civil service system, but became personally dependent on a small but absolutely trustworthy staff of workers, though he retained a few advisors among the old professional diplomats. All decisions were to be made by him. No one was to take any steps unless they had express authority from the Reichsminister himself. Instructions were in great detail and seemed to spring from a deeply rooted mistrust of the ability and even the loyalty of his coworkers. He felt himself personally responsible to Hitler for even the smallest detail. This led to a tremendous amount of work on trivia, about which he said, "I just have to do everything myself." His staff was well taken care of financially and he rewarded them generously after some especially well-done job and at Christmas, according to his secretary. If an injury or illness was suffered by a staff member, as from the bombings, he would send the best doctors, would expect a daily report, and would pay all the expenses. He sent fine presents and granted generous vacations. On the other hand, faithlessness or disloyalty constituted the biggest crimes of all, in his thinking. He would fire loyal, longtime staff members under humiliating conditions, if they violated his trust even in minor ways.

A Diplomat for Peace

As the end neared in April of 1945, several of the top Nazis, including Ribbentrop, made efforts to negotiate with the Western Allies. Hitler was obviously fading away, but would not admit it. The military men were trying to figure out how they could induce the Americans and British to stop the advancing Russians. [High-ranking SS officer Ernst] Kaltenbrunner had contacted [U.S. Chief of the Office of Strategic Services] Allen Dulles's men in Switzerland; [SS chief Heinrich] Himmler also tried to arrange a surrender to the British in April.

Ribbentrop tried to get the Japanese ambassador to pressure Sweden to negotiate a capitulation. The ambassador referred Ribbentrop to the Swedish Count Bernadotte. Bernadotte received Ribbentrop but was subjected to an hour-long, arrogant monologue and withdrew in disgust. Thus Ribbentrop had attempted to join several others in trying to desert the sinking ship.

He hung around [Hitler's successor, Karl] Dönitz's headquarters, dodging the British and Americans until June 14 when an acquaintance turned him in to the British authorities in Hamburg. From there he went directly to our Mondorf Detention Center. He had hidden out the longest of all the defendants.

Profiles · in · History

Engineers of Death

Rudolf Höss: The Death Dealer

Roger Manvell and Heinrich Fraenkel

Rudolf Höss joined the SS (Schutzstaffel, the protection squad for high-ranking Nazis and later the chief policing agency throughout Germany) in 1934. He worked in Dachau and Sachsenhausen concentration camps before becoming the commandant of Auschwitz in 1940. In this position, by his own admission, he orchestrated the murder of 3 million people. In this selection from their book entitled *The Incomparable Crime*, Roger Manvell and Heinrich Fraenkel draw upon transcripts from Höss's trials at the International Military Tribunal at Nuremberg in 1946 and the Supreme National Tribunal in Poland in 1947 in order to portray Höss as a man who recoiled from violence yet fully supported the "Final Solution," the extermination of the Jews. Manvell and Fraenkel theorize that Höss was just an ordinary man who became conditioned to cruelty and thereby became an effective instrument of genocide and mass extermination.

Manvell and Fraenkel are historical researchers who have written prolifically, both together and separately, about Nazi Germany and those who held high-ranking positions within the Nazi Party. Manvell's books include *SS and Gestapo: Rule by Terror*, *Dr. Goebbels*, and *Goering*. Fraenkel is the author of *The German People Versus Hitler*, *Germany's Road to Democracy*, and *Farewell to Germany*.

Roger Manvell and Heinrich Fraenkel, *The Incomparable Crime*. London, UK: William Heinemann, Ltd., 1967. Copyright © 1967 by Roger Manvell and Heinrich Fraenkel. Reproduced by permission of the Literary Estates of Roger Manvell and Heinrich Fraenkel.

Books they have written together include *The July Plot* and *Heinrich Himmler.*

🐞   🐞   🐞

It was a good thing that the father of Rudolf Franz Ferdinand Hoess [Höss], who was made Commandant of Auschwitz at the age of forty, did not live to see what became of his son after the stern, Catholic upbringing to which he had been subjected. Hoess [born in 1900] a man of modest intelligence, has left his own detailed account of his life, written in a Polish prison after the war. In diligent, homely prose he tried to rationalize his own disturbed life; he described a lonely middle-class childhood, his alienation from the demonstrations of affection shown by his mother, an 'exaggerated' love for animals, a passion for water and washing and an unloving veneration for his father, a former soldier who had become a travelling salesman. 'My father had taken a vow that I should be a priest. . . . I was educated entirely with this end in view. My father brought me up on strict military principles. . . . He prayed passionately that the Grace of God might be bestowed upon me'. He died while Hoess was still a boy.

When Dr G.M. Gilbert, American Prison Psychologist at the Nuremberg Trial where Hoess appeared as a witness, questioned him in his cell about his childhood, Hoess said:

> Yes, I was brought up in a very strict Catholic tradition. My father was really a bigot. He was very strict and fanatical. I learned that my father took a religious oath at the time of the birth of my youngest sister, dedicating me to God and the priesthood, and after that leading a celibate married life. He directed my entire youthful education toward the goal of

making me a priest. I had to pray and go to church endlessly, do penance over the slightest misdeed—praying as punishment for any little unkindness to my sister, or something like that.

Soldier and Prisoner

After his father's death, Hoess's ambitions were more for soldiering than religion; he joined the army under age, saw action in Palestine and Jordan, caught malaria, and fell in love with a nurse at the front. He claims that he was the youngest non-commissioned officer in the German army, and he soon became a hardened soldier. By now all ideas of the priesthood were over, though he was still under pressure from his family to attend a training college for priests. He turned his back on his relatives, and became a member of the Nazi Party. He joined the unofficial *Freikorps* Movement—the volunteers from the disbanded German army who were re-formed into fighting units to guard Germany's frontiers—and he discovered more action along the borders of east Prussia and the Baltic States, where he saw civilian families burned to death in their homes.

In 1923 he was involved in a brutal political murder—the victim was beaten almost to death, and then had his throat cut. Hoess was sentenced to ten years' imprisonment. He claimed later to Dr Gilbert that he felt no guilt for his part in this murder because it was political, and for the 'protection of the fatherland'. But it was in prison, he says, that he learned all there was to know about human degradation, and he told Gilbert that life in prison, which included solitary confinement, broadened the gulf between society and his 'withdrawn nature'. He described his experiences there with the shocked air of a village schoolmaster: 'I could never accustom myself to the common, cynical and filthy way in which the prisoners treated everything good and beautiful', he wrote in his memoirs. Later he suffered from prison psychosis. When he had recovered, he decided to study English. In 1928, after five years' imprisonment, he was released; he married in 1929, and became a member of a 'folk' agricultural movement called the *Artamanen*, through which he claims he first made the acquaintance of [S.S. chief Heinrich] Himmler. He joined the S.S. in 1933, and was transferred to the staff of Dachau concentration camp after its formation in 1934. Summoned with other recruits to witness his first whipping, he was, he says, appalled. 'When the man began to scream, I went hot and cold all over'.

Hoess admitted to Dr Gilbert at Nuremberg that he accepted anti-Semitism unquestioningly from the Nazi leadership: 'For me, as an old fanatic National Socialist, I took it all as fact—just as a Catholic believes in his Church dogma'. He never questioned whether the Jews he murdered were in fact guilty or not:

> We S.S. men were not supposed to think about these things; it never even occurred to us. . . . It was something already taken for granted that the Jews were to blame for everything. . . . We just never heard anything else. . . . Our military and ideological training took for granted that we had to protect Germany from the Jews.

He appeared quite apathetic and matter-of-fact, though now that his attention was being drawn to the matter, Gilbert records that he showed 'some belated interest in the enormity of his crime'.

When Gilbert gave Hoess a psychological test, Hoess remarked:

> I suppose you want to know in this way if my thoughts and habits are normal. I am entirely normal. Even while I was doing this extermination work, I led a normal family life. . . . Perhaps it was a peculiarity of mine, but I always felt best when alone.

If I had worries, I tried to work them out myself.
That was the thing that disturbed my wife most: I
was so self-sufficient. I never had friends or a close
relationship with anybody—even in my youth. . . .
Of course, I loved my wife, but a real spiritual
union—that was lacking.

Promotions and Decorations

The manner of Hoess's conditioning for the career he
was so proud to undertake at Auschwitz is of great significance. No other Nazi concerned with extermination . . . has been at once so frank and so revealing in
his rationalizations. . . . Hoess was neither a psychopath
nor a sadist. He belonged to the rank and file of humanity, but a member of the rank and file conditioned
to eliminate all compassion from his nature and behaviour so far as the prisoners he supervised were concerned. In this sense, he became brutalized in the pursuit of duty; although he was always sentimental, he was
utterly insensitive, and he had little difficulty in adapt-
ing himself to the circumstances in which he was placed
and which were soon to favour his rapid promotion. Although his ambition was soldiering, he was considered
an ideal camp guard. In 1935 he became a block-leader
with the rank of S.S. sergeant; in 1936, he was promoted S.S. sergeant-major. As the result of a strong
recommendation from his superiors, he became later in
the year a second-lieutenant, and was moved to take
charge of stores at Sachsenhausen concentration camp.
In 1939 he became Commandant of Sachsenhausen
Camp. The following year he was given the responsible
task of forming the new camp at Auschwitz in Poland.
From 1943 he served in Berlin in the S.S. Head Office
with the rank of lieutenant-colonel, and was awarded
the War Service Cross I, with swords. . . .

Hoess admitted later that his personal guilt began [af-
ter becoming a concentration camp commandant]. He

felt unsuited for the work, but did not have the courage
to say so. Instead, he cultivated a 'stony mask' to hide
what he claimed to be his sympathy with the prisoners.
Also, he says that he 'had become too fond of the black
uniform to relinquish it'. He dared not risk discharge
and the loss of face. In any case, he believed in Hitler, in
the S.S. and in the concentration-camp system. On the
other hand, he claims that he 'disagreed with the way he
[First Commandant of Dachau, S.S. Colonel Theodor
Eicke] whipped up the vilest emotions of hatred among
the S.S. guards, and with his policy of putting incompe-
tent men in charge of the prisoners and of allowing
these unsuitable, indeed intolerable, persons to keep
their jobs'. Eicke thought him efficient and promoted
him Adjutant at Sachsenhausen.

Hoess's inner scruples 'receded into the background'
now that he no longer came into 'such direct contact
with the prisoners'. There were subordinates and Kapos
[prisoners chosen to head work gangs of other prisoners]
to do the worst of the work. The rot had set in. Hitler
seemed all-powerful in Europe in 1938, and Hoess had
learnt by then that 'in the S.S. hard necessity must stifle
all softer emotions'. He even had to command the firing
squad which carried out sentence on an S.S. officer condemned to death for affording a kindness to a prisoner,
which had led to an escape. The moral was not lost on
Hoess, whose own good fortune seemed to have reached
its height when Himmler gave him the opportunity in
1940 to found the new camp at Auschwitz in Poland. He
went there in May, with the rank of S.S. captain. . . .

Then, in the summer of 1941, 'by the will of the
Reichsführer S.S., Auschwitz became the greatest extermination centre of all time'.

Reflecting on the orders he received, Hoess wrote:

> When in the summer of 1941 he [Himmler] himself
> gave me the order to prepare installations at Auschwitz

where mass exterminations could take place, and personally to carry out these exterminations, I did not have the slightest idea of their scale or consequences. It was certainly an extraordinary and monstrous order. Nevertheless the reasons behind the extermination programme seemed to me right. I did not reflect on it at the time: I had been given an order, and I had to carry it out. Whether this mass extermination of the Jews was necessary or not was something on which I could not allow myself to form an opinion, for I lacked the necessary breadth of view. . . . Since my arrest it has been said to me repeatedly that I could have disobeyed this order, and that I might even have assassinated Himmler. I do not believe that of all the thousands of S.S. officers there could have been found a single one capable of such a thought. It was completely impossible. Certainly many S.S. officers grumbled and complained about some of the harsh orders that came from the Reichsführer S.S., but they nevertheless always carried them out.

Before the International Military Tribunal

On 15 April 1946, Hoess was called as a witness before the International Military Tribunal at Nuremberg. Here, without flinching, he made statements more appalling than any man has ever made before in a court of law. He spoke throughout, says Gilbert, in his usual quiet, apathetic, matter-of-fact tone of voice. . . .

Under cross-examination by Colonel John Amen, one of the American counsels, Hoess confirmed in court the facts to which he had already sworn in the form of an affidavit. Passages from this affidavit were read out by Colonel Amen, and the court sat silent and horrified as they listened to these cold, summary words:

COLONEL AMEN: I will omit the first paragraph and start with paragraph 2:

'I have been constantly associated with the administration of concentration camps since 1934, serving at

Dachau until 1938; then as Adjutant in Sachsenhausen from 1938 to May 1st, 1940, when I was appointed Commandant of Auschwitz. I commanded Auschwitz until 1st December, 1943, and estimate that at least 2,500,000 victims were executed and exterminated there by gassing and burning, and at least another half million succumbed to starvation and disease making a total dead of about 3,000,000. This figure represents about 70 per cent or 80 per cent of all persons sent to Auschwitz as prisoners, the remainder having been selected and used for slave labour in the concentration-camp industries. Included among the executed and burnt were approximately 20,000 Russian prisoners of war (previously selected and taken out of prisoner-of-war cages by the Gestapo) who were delivered to Auschwitz in Wehrmacht transports operated by regular Wehrmacht officers and men. The remainder of the total number of victims included about 100,000 German Jews, and great numbers of citizens, mostly Jewish, from Holland, France, Belgium, Poland, Hungary, Czechoslovakia, Greece, or other countries. We executed about 400,000 Hungarian Jews alone at Auschwitz in the summer of 1944'.

That is all true, witness?

HOESS: Yes, it is. . . .

AMEN: 'The "final solution" of the Jewish question meant the complete extermination of all Jews in Europe. I was ordered to establish extermination facilities at Auschwitz in June 1941. At that time, there were already three other extermination camps in the Government General: Belzec, Treblinka and Wolzek. These camps were under the *Einsatzkommando* [operations unit] of the Security Police and S.D. [*Sicherheitsdienst*, the security branch of the S.S.]. I visited Treblinka to find out how they carried out their extermination. The Camp Commandant at Treblinka told me that he had liquidated 80,000 in the course of half a year. He was principally concerned with liquidating all the Jews from the Warsaw Ghetto. He used monoxide gas, and I did not think that his methods were very efficient. So when I set up the extermination building at Auschwitz, I used Cyclon B, which was a crystallized prussic acid which we dropped into the death chamber from a small opening. It took from 3 to 15 minutes to kill the people in the death chamber, depending upon climatic conditions. We knew when the people were dead because their screaming stopped. We usually waited about half an hour before we opened the doors and removed the bodies. After the bodies were removed our special commandos took off the rings and extracted the gold from the teeth of the corpses'.

Is that all true and correct, witness?

HOESS: Yes. . . .

AMEN: 'Another improvement we made as compared with Treblinka was that we built our gas chamber to accommodate 2,000 people at one time whereas at Treblinka their 10 gas chambers only accommodated 200 people each. The way we selected our victims was as follows: we had two S.S. doctors on duty at Auschwitz to examine the incoming transports of prisoners. The prisoners would be marched past one of the doctors who would make 'spot' decisions as they walked by. Those who were fit for work were sent into the camp. Others were sent immediately to the extermination plants. Children of tender years were invariably exterminated since, by reason of their youth, they were unable to work. At Treblinka the victims almost always knew that they were to be exterminated. We followed a better policy at Auschwitz by endeavouring to fool the victims into thinking that they were to go through a delousing process. Of course, frequently they realized our true intentions and we sometimes had riots and difficulties due to that fact. Very frequently women would hide their children under their clothes, but of course when we found them we would send the children in to be exterminated. We were required to carry out these exterminations in secrecy but naturally the foul and nauseating stench from the continuous burning of bodies permeated the entire area and all of the people living in the surrounding districts knew that exterminations were going on at Auschwitz'.

Is that all true and correct, witness?

HOESS: Yes.

. . . With a nice eye for detail, Hoess recounts story after story to show how the Jews sensed they were going to their deaths and failed to keep the peace. Throughout his written confession, he does not attempt to conceal his contempt for the Jews. The worst of the work was handed over, he claims, to other Jewish prisoners formed into commandos responsible to their S.S. masters for handling the corpses:

> The bodies had to be taken from the gas chambers, and after the gold teeth had been extracted, and the hair cut off, they had to be dragged to the pits or to the crematoria. Then the fires in the pits had to be stoked, the surplus fat drained off, and the mountain of burning corpses constantly turned over so that the draught might fan the flames. They carried out all these tasks with a callous indifference as though it were all part of an ordinary day's work.

Hoess can only conclude from this that the Jews appeared to be an utterly callous people. 'The Jew's way of living and dying was a true riddle that I never managed to solve', is how he puts it.

A Mandate for Extermination

For the record, Hoess claims that he was moved by what he had to do. 'We were all tormented by secret doubts', he said. But, as Commandant, it was his duty to 'exercise intense self-control. . . . I had to go on with this process of extermination. I had to continue this mass murder and coldly watch it. . . . I had to observe every happening with cold indifference. . . . In Auschwitz I truly had no reason to complain that I was bored'. When the work became too oppressive, Hoess would mount his horse 'and ride until I had chased the terrible picture away. . . . I could no longer bear to be in my homely family circle. When I saw my children happily playing, or observed my wife's delight over our youngest, the thought would often come to me: how long will our happiness last? My wife could never understand these gloomy moods of mine. . . . I was no longer happy in Auschwitz once the mass exterminations had begun. I had become dissatisfied with myself'.

Hoess ends his confession with a number of extraordinary statements:

> I have described myself as I was and as I am. I have lived a full and varied life. I have followed my star wherever it led me. Life has given me some hard and rough knocks, but I have always managed to get along. I have never given in. . . . I regarded the National-Socialist attitude to the world as the only one suited to the German people. . . . Unknowingly I was a cog in the wheel of the great extermination machine created by the Third Reich. The machine has been smashed to pieces, the engine is broken and I, too, must now be destroyed. The world demands it. . . . Let the public continue to regard me as the bloodthirsty beast, the cruel sadist and the mass murderer; for the masses could never imagine the Commandant of Auschwitz in any other light. They could never understand that he, too, had a heart and that he was not evil.

The Monstrous Work of a Small Man

Hoess stood trial before the Supreme National Tribunal in Poland during March 1947. Here he admitted yet again: 'I am responsible for everything that happened at Auschwitz'. He disputed only the details, claiming that he himself signed no execution orders, fired no shots. Hermann Langbein, who came from Austria to testify, claimed that Hoess acted like a 'government robot, yet took personal pleasure in carrying out the general plan of extermination and himself organized an entire series of sadistic actions'. Witness after witness testified to the nature of Auschwitz; one said, 'the odour of burning flesh made one lose faith in humanity and justice'. The continuous cruelty imposed on the prisoners at Auschwitz, quite apart from the fact that they were condemned to extermination, must be regarded as the particular responsibility of Hoess. The Polish prosecutor, Siewierski, in his final speech to the Tribunal indicted Hoess from the standpoint of both reason and morality, since, as he put it, 'no anger or violence against Hoess could compensate for the evil done by him'. Hoess was condemned to death. He was taken to Auschwitz and hanged there on 15 April 1947.

It is strange that Hoess was content to allow mankind to remember him as a monster. The image of the evildoer demands a painted devil which is larger than life, the monstrous inhumanity of a Mephisto [from Johann von Goethe's drama *Faust*], the motiveless malignity of an Iago [from William Shakespeare's *Othello*]. Hoess, knowing himself in reality to be a small man, instinctively preferred to die under the great shadow of his notoriety. It gave romantic stature to his evil-doing.

But, like Himmler, he has little personal, as distinct from social and historical, significance. The lesson of Auschwitz is that the unparalleled crime of genocide committed there was undertaken by small and seemingly ordinary men doing what they conceived to be their duty with the lusty help of many criminals and a few psychopaths, together with the forced labour, both willing and unwilling, recruited from among the prisoners themselves.

Josef Mengele: The Angel of Death

Louis L. Snyder

At the beginning of World War II, Josef Mengele (born in 1911), a medical doctor, enlisted in the Waffen SS (the branch of the SS that assisted the German army) and served as a medical officer in France and Russia. In 1942 Mengele was promoted by Heinrich Himmler to chief physician at Auschwitz, where his well-documented medical experiments earned him the title "Angel of Death." Mengele disappeared in the postwar years, then surfaced in South America, pursued by Nazi hunters Simon Wiesenthal and Beate Klarsfeld. In June 1985 the *New York Post* wire service reported that the skeletal remains found in a coffin in Brazil were believed to be those of Mengele. In this selection from *The Nazi Elite: Shocking Profiles of the Reich's Most Notorious Henchmen*, Louis L. Snyder portrays Mengele as cold, calculating, and indifferent to the human suffering that he was trained to alleviate. Snyder also describes Mengele's postwar years as a fugitive and the international search to find him.

Snyder's extensive knowledge of World War II–era Germany stems from the years he spent as a German American exchange student at the University of Frankfurt-am-Main prior to World War II. During the same time period Snyder served as a special correspondent from Germany for the Paris edition of the *New York Herald*. During a career that spanned almost seventy years, Snyder wrote nearly sixty books, most of them about Nazi Germany. His other books include *The Nazi Elite: Biographical Sketches of Nazis Who Shaped the Third Reich*, *Encyclopedia of the Third Reich*, and *Hitler and Naziism*.

❦   ❦   ❦

Among Hitler's medicine men was Dr. Josef Mengele, head physician at Auschwitz, whose specialty was what he called the science of twins. The doctor's goal was the artificial creation of Aryan children distinguished by blond hair and fair features—the type favored by the *Fuehrer*. Mengele was known among camp inmates as "the collector of blue eyes."

Josef Mengele was born on March 16, 1911, in Günzburg, a quaint medieval town of some twelve thousand inhabitants on the banks of the Danube in Bavaria. His father founded the farm-machinery factory of Karl Mengele and Sons, an enterprise employing many townspeople. The family was noted both for its wealth and its public spirit. Soon after World War I the Mengele business acquired an interest in an assembly plant in Buenos Aires, Argentina. That move was to be of critical importance later for Dr. Mengele when he fled from prosecution after World War II.

A Follower of Rosenberg

Young Josef was regarded with pride by the Mengele clan. He showed promise as a student and much was expected of him. In the mid-1920s he went to Munich to study philosophy. There he was attracted by the racial ideology of Alfred Rosenberg, up-and-coming philosopher of the Nazi movement. He also met budding politician Hitler. He soon became a fanatical follower of the Nazi chieftain.

The young man was bothered by one annoying problem. Though he praised the Aryan "race," he, himself, was short, swarthy, and dark complexioned, just the opposite of the tall, blond Nordic superman he worshipped. Because he was often mistaken for a Gypsy, he developed a lifelong bitter hatred for the wandering, dark-skinned people. He was trapped by his physical appearance—and there was no way he could change it.

Mengele moved from Munich to Frankfurt-am-Main, where he attended the university and took a degree in medicine. He had a vague idea of combining interests in both philosophy and medicine. In common with Alfred Rosenberg's idea of racial superiority, he developed a theory that human beings, like dogs, had distinct pedigrees. This became the basis for his later experimentation designed to breed a race of Nordic-Aryan giants.

In the early months of World War II Mengele enlisted in the armed forces, for which he served in the *Waffen-SS* as an *Untersturmfuehrer* (2nd lieutenant). He was initially assigned to France as a medical officer and later to the Russian front. In 1943 he received an important promotion when [SS leader] Heinrich Himmler appointed him chief physician at extermination camp Auschwitz.

The deterioration of Auschwitz had already begun when Mengele was sent there to supervise its medical facilities. Situated on a marshy tract between the Vistula and tributary Sola, the camp was surrounded by stagnant and smelly ponds. Originally housing a military barracks, it was later the site of a tobacco factory. Under Commandant Rudolf Hoess, hundreds of thousands of prisoners were executed in this hell hole. Many others were allowed to starve to death.

Conditions in Auschwitz were chaotic. Inmates died of malnutrition and illnesses, including typhus, diarrhea, typhoid fever, and tuberculosis. It was a nightmare for any normal physician. There were sickening scenes in the compound. Prisoners, reacting like dogs, lapped up what little food they could find. Their only source of water was next to the latrines. They fought for a taste of water while their fellow sufferers sat in the latrines next to them. Hardened guards, including females, lashed out with clubs on the inmates. *SS* officers looked on with cold indifference. . . .

A Medical Murderer

This was the atmosphere into which the good Dr. Mengele settled to do his stint for the glory of the Third Reich. Long forgotten was the normal physician's concern for people in trouble. He was now chief of a medical staff of ten men and they had a job to do.

Ten men. Ten doctors. Few were convinced Nazis or fanatical anti-Semites—except Mengele. Most had little taste for the work they were required to do. But they deemed it to their own best interest to obey. The authorities (*die Obrigkeit*) had issued orders, and it was their duty to do what they were told to do. Most of the ten, upset by their assignment, remained continually drunk.

But not Dr. Mengele. Eyewitnesses reported that he was always sober—even under the most horrifying conditions. He took delight in ending the lives of those he believed unfit to live under National Socialism. It was a pleasure to get rid of biologically impure Jews and Gypsies. Especially Gypsies. Why had an unkind fate given him a physical appearance so close to that of a people he scorned?

The man later described as a medical murderer was a stickler for neatness and cleanliness. He strode around the compound in immaculate uniform, carefully pressed, with shiny boots and white gloves. He had a habit of keeping his thumb in his pistol belt. His private office was impeccably clean. He could smile at an innocent while giving a lethal injection with a carefully disinfected syringe. . . .

The Selector

Spotless Mengele and his nine assistants were responsible for the selective process which meant the difference between life and death for prisoners. First came the Canada Detail, composed of inmates trained to handle incoming prisoners. Meeting arriving transports, they searched the victims for booty. They also cleaned the filthy railroad wagons and then loaded them with anything of value taken from the prisoners. One report told how in February 1943 exactly 781 wagonloads filled with booty left Auschwitz for Germany; 245 were filled with clothing, others with human hair and gold fillings extracted from the mouths of executed prisoners.

After the work of the Canada Detail came the selective medical process. Dr. Mengele, anxious not to miss any important assignment, was always there day and night. He and assistants Drs. König, Thile, and Klein, among others, took part in this elaborate charade. Their main task was to select prisoners for the industrial machine. Those fit to work ("positive selection") were separated from those too weak or ill for manual labor. The scene was one of grotesque and ultimate cruelty. Victims were paraded before the doctors for instant decisions. In the spot selection "Right" meant work in the factories—and life itself. "Left" was the word of doom—removal to subcamp Birkenau and its gas ovens.

The prisoners chosen to go left were immediately deprived of their luggage. Then came separation of men and women. The unfortunates were led to an area where they could see great flames belching from chimneys and could smell the odor of what was called the "bakery." Some believed the large sign: "WASH AND DISINFECTING ROOMS." Guards who collected clothing and valuables always gave careful receipts. Women had their hair cut off. The irregular lines were then led to the "disinfecting rooms."

A Murderer of Children and Gypsies

Inmates throughout the camp were terrified of Dr. Mengele and his small band of killer-physicians. An eyewitness later recalled that in October 1944 Mengele, leading the selective process with other officers, came to Barracks 11, where presumably healthy Jewish children between the ages of sixteen and eighteen were housed. "They probably sensed what they were in for and dispersed. Thereupon the camp leader rounded them up like dogs. That happened on a Jewish holiday. After two days vans came, and the boys were put in the vans and taken to the gas chambers. This was done amidst laughter. They were probably amazed because these children cried out for their mothers."

Other witnesses gave additional details about Mengele's behavior at Auschwitz. Hermann Langbehn, a Viennese, later general secretary of the International Auschwitz Committee, worked there as a clerk. He told how Mengele and other camp officials kept precise records: day and night, in shifts at seven typewriters, clerks filled out forms with notations of day and hour of death on file cards. Records were considered to be far more important than lives.

Nazi hunter [and Auschwitz survivor] Simon Wiesenthal interviewed Langbehn about Mengele's work at Auschwitz: "Langbehn told me that once Mengele came into the children's block at Auschwitz to measure the boys' height. He became very angry when he found many of them too small for their age. He made the boys stand against a doorpost marked with nails for each group. If the boy's head did not reach the proper nail, Mengele gave a sign with his riding crop. The child was taken away to the gas chambers. More than a thousand children were murdered at that time."

The very sight of Gypsies aroused Mengele to fury. He decided eventually to liquidate the entire Gypsy compound. What happened was described by seventy-one-year-old Maximilian Sternol, who testified at a post-war trial: "On the night of July 31, 1944, there were terrible scenes at the Gypsy compound. Women and children were on their knees before Mengele and Boger, crying 'Take pity on us, take pity on us!' Nothing helped. They were beaten down, brutally trampled upon, and pushed into the trucks. It was a terrible, gruesome sight."

Medical Experimenter

Mengele had his own special solutions for camp problems. When he came to Auschwitz, he found six hundred sick women in 180 beds in the hospital barracks. Most were plagued with lice, carriers of typhus. Mengele did not hesitate. He met the problem by gassing the entire block. He then disinfected the area, put in a bathtub, and allowed inmates of an adjoining block to bathe there.

Some charges against Mengele seem incredible. One witness informed Wiesenthal that he had seen the doctor throw a baby alive into a fire. Another swore that Mengele killed a fourteen-year-old girl with a bayonet.

Mengele kept himself busy at Auschwitz with his own race purification program. He would win the *Fuehrer*'s eternal gratitude by his work in promoting a race of biologically superior Nordic men and women. Collecting corpses of what he called subhumans, he sent them to the Institute for Racial Biology in Berlin for further examination. Most important for him was his specialty of medical experimentation on twins to find a means of multiplying the population of the German nation. He was accused of supervising an operation by which two Gypsy children were sewn together to create Siamese twins. The purpose of the procedure was not entirely clear. Its only result was said to be that the hands of the children became badly infected where their veins had been resected.

Postwar Obscurity
Using skills he had learned in tracking other Nazis, Wiesenthal found that at the end of the war Mengele had gone home to Günzburg. Here, Mengele's relatives and friends, unaware of his ghastly work at Auschwitz, greeted him as a returned war hero. The doctor had done his duty for his country. Although Günzburg was in the U.S. Zone of Occupation, American authorities apparently knew nothing about Mengele's record.

For five years Mengele remained in the old Bavarian town. He made occasional visits to nearby Munich. Then his name began to emerge again and again during trials of Nazis for war crimes. Testimony taken at these trials revealed much about his activities at Auschwitz.

By this time Mengele thought it expedient to disappear. Like other wanted Nazis, he turned to ODESSA, the secret escape organization of the *SS* underground, a clandestine travel bureau set up to enable former *SS* officers to avoid arrest by the Allies. The most favored terminal point was Buenos Aires in Argentina. The usual escape route was Italy-Spain–South America.

In 1952 Mengele, fortified with a set of false identity papers, arrived in Buenos Aires. Posing as Dr. Friedrich Edler von Breitenbach, he set up a practice as a physician-without-license. He was not especially worried because he was on good terms with dictator [Juan] Perón's police. Later, he assumed a large number of pseudonyms, including Helmut Gregor-Gregori, Fausto Rindon, José Aspiazi, Sebastian Alvez, Walter Hŭsek, Heinz Stobert, Fritz Fischer, and Lars Balistroem. He was advised by ODESSA officials to change his identity as often as possible. He hoped to sink into anonymity and escape the vengeance of those who had not forgotten what he had done at Auschwitz.

There was danger in the air for Mengele. When Perón was overthrown and went into exile in September 1955, Mengele and many of his Nazi comrades began to fear for their own safety. The once easily-bribed Argentine authorities were now gone; there were problems about remaining in the country. Most Nazis residing in Buenos Aires began moving to Paraguay, especially to capital city Asunción. Mengele was among them. Finding it dangerous to practice medicine illegally, he, instead, took over management of his family's local business office.

Germany Gives Up the Search

Meanwhile, Mengele's work at Auschwitz was being fully documented in German courts. Authorities of the Federal Republic, sensitive to its reputation, offered a reward of 60,000 marks (at that time worth about $16,000) for his capture. Nazi-hunter Wiesenthal, never forgetting the search for Mengele, urged Bonn [German] authorities to demand extradition. The German officials were willing to bring him back for trial. Early in January 1960 an urgent request was sent from Bonn to Argentina for Mengele's extradition.

The German Embassy in Buenos Aires was told to pursue the matter. It soon ran into a stone wall. The Argentine *Procurador de la Nación* [Solicitor of the Nation (Attorney General)] informed embassy officials that Mengele's offenses were political rather than criminal. Admittedly, he said, the evidence against the doctor was impressive, but it was not his place to overcome the psychological attitude throughout South America, which made extradition virtually impossible. Mengele, after all, was a "guest," and even though he had a dark past it was not in the interest of Argentina to grant the request. Faced with this tortuous reasoning, the German officials gave up in disgust.

Meanwhile, Mengele returned to Paraguay where, aided by influential friends, he managed to obtain Paraguayan citizenship. He disappeared in Bariloche, a resort in the lake district of the Andes, where many wealthy Nazis had settled on large estates. The area, close to the borders of Chile, provided means for a further escape in case of necessity.

Authorities in Argentina belatedly took additional interest in Mengele. In June 1960 they issued a warrant for his arrest. It was too late. The doctor-on-the-run moved into Brazil. Once again he disappeared.

From Brazil, Mengele fled to Cairo and then to a Greek island. Again he returned to the safe haven in Paraguay, whose authorities notified Bonn that he was a citizen "with no criminal record." All efforts to obtain his extradition to Germany were unsuccessful. Paraguay's President, General Alfredo Stroessner, threatened to break off diplomatic relations with the Federal Republic of West Germany if it persisted in its efforts for Mengele's extradition.

There was a complicating factor for the Paraguayan government. It was interested in obtaining a three-million dollar development loan from Bonn. Hence, it decided to delay a decision on Mengele. He was isolated in a heavily guarded area of eastern Paraguay, where no foreigners were permitted. Interpol, the international police agency, indicated that it would like to get its hands on Mengele, but Paraguay was not a member of that organization.

The wanted doctor had escaped retribution from both the Bonn Republic and Israel, but he was not altogether a free man. Wiesenthal described Mengele's life in Paraguay . . .

> Mengele now lives as a virtual prisoner in the restricted military zone between Puerto San Vincente on the Asunció–Sao Paolo highway and the border fortress of Carlos Antonio López on the Paraná River. Here he occupies a small white shed in a jungle area cleared by German settlers. Only two roads lead to the secluded house. Both are patrolled by Portuguese soldiers and police, who have strict orders to stop all cars and shoot all trespassers. And just in case the police should slip up, there are four heavily armed private bodyguards with radios and walkie-talkies. Mengele pays for them himself.

Despite Wiesenthal's report, Paraguayan authorities continued to deny that they knew of Mengele's whereabouts. The Minister of the Interior and the head of the Supreme Court asserted that he could not be found. In late February 1984 a criminal judge in Asunción, Anselmo Aveiro, reissued a 22-year-old order for the arrest of the Nazi fugitive.

Another Nazi pursuer [Beate Klarsfeld] joined the hunt. . . .

The search for Mengele was yielding no results. In 1979, under pressure from abroad, the Paraguayan Supreme Court had stripped him of his citizenship. That year one report had it that he had flown from Asunción to Miami. From 1981 to 1985 checks on his whereabouts were made in Miami, West Germany, as well as in Paraguay, Chile, Brazil, Ecuador, Bolivia, Uruguay, Australia, and other countries. No success. . . .

Late Bulletins, 1985

Embu, Brazil (The New York Post Wire Services, June 7, 1985). Gravediggers yesterday smashed open a coffin

that investigators believe may contain the body of the
Nazi "Angel of Death" Dr. Josef Mengele, the world's
most wanted fugitive.

Sao Paulo, Brazil (Associated Press, June 8, 1985). Coro-
ners yesterday began cleaning the bones unearthed in a
nearby town to determine whether they belong to Josef
Mengele, the infamous Angel of Death in the Nazi concentration camp at Auschwitz.

Time, July 1, 1985. The 16 forensic experts (six of
them American) who have been examining the skeletal
remains announced their unanimous conclusion: "The
skeleton is that of Josef Mengele within a reasonable
scientific certainty." Later, the Americans reported that
they had "absolutely no doubt" of their findings.

The extraordinary search for Josef Mengele was supposed to have ended in this way. But serious doubts still
existed as to whether the bones and teeth really were the
remains of the notorious camp doctor. Some observers
believe that it was useless to keep hunting for the old
man who once ran Hitler's murder machine. The evil
empire lay buried and its former servants now posed no
further threat. Even if the barbarous Angel of Death
were still alive, they say, it is as a reclusive fugitive.

Others disagree. It does matter, they insist, that the
escaped murderer be traced down. To shrug him off as
a harmless old man would be to condone his crimes and
to evade the world's debt to his victims. The man was
an example of the indifferent boorishness that was the
public face of Nazism. This point of view remains—the
butchers must be hunted to the end of their days.

Adolf Eichmann: The Embodiment of Evil

Charles Ashman and Robert J. Wagman

Adolf Eichmann was raised in Austria. When he was twenty-six years old, he joined the Austrian National Socialist Party as a member of the SS (Schutzstaffel), the protection squad for high-ranking Nazis that became the chief policing agency throughout Germany. Later he became associated with the SD (Sicherheitsdienst), the branch of the SS involved in security work, where his talents for bureaucracy were noted. Eichmann took it upon himself to research Jews and Judaism, activities that brought him to the attention of higher-ranking Nazis as a "Jewish specialist." In 1938, after the Anschluss (Germany's reunification of Austria), Eichmann became the director of the Office for Jewish Emigration in Vienna, the only Nazi agency authorized to issue exit permits to Jews from Germany and German-occupied countries. Eichmann later was instrumental in implementing procedures that led to the deaths of millions by his mobile killing units, the SS Einsatz, forcing Jews into overcrowded, unsanitary ghettos, and organizing the transport of Jews to concentration camps. Caught by the Allies at the conclusion of World War II, Eichmann escaped from a U.S. prisoner-of-war camp and fled to Argentina in 1946.

In the following excerpt from their book *The Nazi Hunters*, Charles Ashman and Robert J. Wagman give an overview of Eichmann's crimes, his years of hiding, and his capture by the Israelis in 1960. Eichmann was put on trial in Israel and was executed in 1961.

Ashman has worked as a United Nations correspondent for the *Sunday Times of London*. He is the author of *Diplomatic Crime*. Wagman, the author of six investigative books, including *Lord's Justice: The Story of the Dalkin Shield*, and a biography of Hubert Humphrey, has worked as a Washington correspondent as well as a syndicated columnist. Together they have also written *Nazi Hunters: Behind the Worldwide Search for Nazi War Criminals*. Ashman's and Wagman's work in the field of hunting Nazis has influenced the United Nations and helped to bring about a UN war crime archive.

❧   ❧   ❧

From the day the war ended, Eichmann had been the most-hunted. If any single individual can be said to be the architect of the Final Solution, it was Eichmann. He was not a personal killer, he was a bureaucrat. He did not personally shoot a gun or operate a gas oven, or stand guard over a prisoner. But, as head of the Gestapo's "Jewish Section," he was the man who put the entire system together and made it work. He took the crazed idea of attaining racial purity by genocide and turned it into a still more crazed reality. He built the camps, he organized the deportations of the Jews to them, he experimented until he found the quickest, cheapest, and most efficient method of mass murder.

Eichmann was born in 1906 at Solingen, in the Rhineland. In 1914 he moved with his family to Linz, Austria, where his father had taken a job as an accountant with a power company. Later, the senior Eichmann went into business for himself, operating a mine that extracted oil from shale. Adolf Eichmann, who was not a good student, dropped out of technical school at the age of fifteen and went to work in his father's mine. He soon left to take a job with the power company, first as an apprentice and, later, as a salesman for a subsidiary oil company establishing gasoline service stations.

In 1932 Eichmann joined the SS. He was recruited by Ernst Kaltenbrunner, a young lawyer who was the son of a former business partner of his father's. Eventually, Kaltenbrunner became head of the SS: he was tried and hanged at Nuremberg. Eichmann was assigned to the Austrian Legion, in which he served in several quasi-military assignments until 1935, when he was transferred to Berlin and assigned to the office that oversaw the activities of Freemasons. Shortly after he arrived in Berlin, the SS set up the Office for Jewish Emigration, to which Eichmann was transferred. The new office was charged with formulating policies toward Jews and overseeing their implementation. After the *Anschluss* [the annexation of Austria by Germany] Eichmann was assigned to the Vienna branch.

In October 1939, one month after World War II began, Adolf Eichmann issued a memorandum outlining the Reich's plan to transport Vienna's Jews to Polish and Czechoslovakian "resettlements," establishing a separate Jewish Territory that would eventually contain the entire population of Jews under German control. The first transport of 1,000 Viennese Jews left on October 20, 1939, for Nisko, Poland. The Central Office in Vienna had gathered the city's Jews into one central organization, which was charged with the task of administering the transports. By assigning the task of running the transports to the Jews themselves, the Germans cleverly served their own ends while giving the operation an appearance of cooperation from within the Jewish community. The Nazi description of these "resettlements" was pure deception. The transports, ostensibly delivering the Jews to a new, autonomous homeland, actually discharged their passengers into a wasteland that offered little or no chance for survival. The Final Solution had begun.

After his success at running the Jewish offices in Vienna and, later, in Prague, Eichmann had been recalled to Berlin, where he was placed in charge of the Reich Center for Jewish Emigration. Later, at Nuremberg, his name was mentioned with great frequency. Several witnesses testified that they had been there the day Eichmann bragged, "I will leap into my grave laughing, because the feeling I have five million human beings on my conscience is for me a source of extraordinary satisfaction."

Eichmann Is Found in Argentina

On May 23, 1960, [Israeli] Premier David Ben-Gurion announced to the world that Adolf Eichmann, the SS Colonel who had headed the Gestapo's Jewish Section, was under arrest in Israel and would stand trial for his life. Ben-Gurion made the announcement before the Knesset (Israel's Parliament) with what *The New York Times* called "dramatic understatement."

No information was given as to where, when, or under what circumstances Eichmann was apprehended and how he had ended up in Israel. When pressed, specifically about whether he had been captured by an agency of Israel or a free-lance Nazi hunter, Ben-Gurion would say no more than "Adolf Eichmann is already under arrest in Israel and will shortly be placed on trial here under the terms of the law for the trial of Nazis and their collaborators."

By the next day, May 24, canvasses of every nation had

convinced the media that there had been no formal extradition from another country. Since it was impossible to believe that a repentant Eichmann had walked across the border and said "I'm here," speculation was that he had been spirited away from wherever he was hiding. Some said that he had been found in the Middle East, others speculated about various South American countries. The following day, with the mystery unresolved, a clean-shaven fifty-three-year-old Adolf Eichmann was arraigned before Chief Magistrate Yedidya Levy in Jaffa.

The judge said, "Adolf Eichmann, you are charged with causing the death of millions of Jews in Germany and the enemy-occupied countries in the years 1938 to 1945. Are you Adolf Eichmann?"

Eichmann turned pale, but remained calm and said in a clear voice, "*Ich vin Adolf Eichmann*" (I am Adolf Eichmann).

Years in Hiding

The Eichmann kidnaping has been immortalized in print and on film, but the complete story of how he was eventually caught has never been made public. Based on details that came out at his trial and later, and discussions we have had with former senior Israeli intelligence officers, we believe we now know most of what happened.

The first indication that Eichmann might be living in Argentina came to the Israelis via the West German secret service. A former Dachau [concentration camp] inmate, living in a Buenos Aires suburb, had reported to Frankfurt prosecutor Fritz Bauer, a dedicated Nazi hunter, that a schoolmate of his daughter, one Nikolaus Klement, had been making violently anti-Semitic statements. The informant suspected that the boy's father, known as Ricardo Klement, a balding, middle-aged office worker who lived in the suburb of Olivos with his German wife and four children, might be a hidden Nazi.

The Israelis became very interested, because the suspect's name was so close to "Ricardo Clementi," an alias known to have been used by one of thirty major Nazis who had fled Europe through Italy and Spain, using Red Cross travel documents obtained through the Vatican.[1]

Eichmann Is Put Under Surveillance

The Israelis did not realize immediately that the unimposing office worker in South America was Eichmann, the killer whom they wanted so badly, but they believed that he was an important Nazi. Israel had no extradition treaty, and only a tenuous relationship, with Argentina. But, with German help, intense negotiations with the Argentine foreign ministry were undertaken. Despite all that would be said later, high-level Argentine officials gave Israeli intelligence operatives permission to put Klement under surveillance.

Once the Israelis got a good look at the suspect, and took photographs that were flown back to Israel and Germany, they began to suspect that Klement was Eichmann. But they were not certain until March 21, 1960, when operatives watched Klement leave work and stop

---

1. It would be learned later that Eichmann had been captured not once, but twice, by the Americans in 1945–46. In the spring of 1945, he had obtained identification papers for himself in the name of Adolf Barth, a Luftwaffe corporal. As the Reich fell, he made his way to Ulm with the false papers and was arrested by the Americans, who released him because they had no interest in low-level members of the regular German army. In early 1946 he was picked up again and sent to a POW camp at Weiden. This time he escaped before his identity could be established.

In March 1946, as Otto Heninger, Eichmann took refuge in Bavaria, where he worked as a logger. Over the next four years, he worked in northern Germany and in Spain, both as a logger, and, for a time, as a chicken farmer. In the spring of 1950, he traveled from Spain to Austria and crossed the Italian border. He obtained the Italian Red Cross displaced-person travel document issued by the Vatican in the name of Clementi.

In Argentina Eichmann worked as a surveyor for an engineering firm. Then he lived under various aliases in Brazil, Paraguay, and Bolivia, doing office work, managing a small laundry, and running a rabbit farm. In 1956 he moved back to Argentina, adopted the name Klement, and worked as a mechanic. Later he spent almost two years in the interior as a farm manager. Apparently, he had been back in the capital, working in a Daimler-Benz auto plant office, for only a short time before he came to the attention of the Germans and Israelis.

at a florist shop to pick up a large bouquet of flowers. They followed him to a new house that he had built, in which he had lived for less than a month, and saw him give the flowers to his wife, who greeted him at the door with a kiss. The watchers were convinced: March 21 was Adolf Eichmann's wedding anniversary.

The Israelis then consulted with German officials. The West German government wanted Eichmann badly, but its previous requests for extradition of Nazis from Argentina had largely been ignored. Despite the Argentine agreement to allow surveillance, the West Germans were not at all confident that a request for Eichmann's return to Germany would meet with success. Rather, it was likely that he would flee and go underground as soon as he learned he had been located. Israel decided that independent action was the only answer.

The Israelis considered assassination, but dismissed the idea. As [Nazi hunter] Simon Wiesenthal has said, "if you kill an Eichmann, the world will never learn what he did." There had to be a trial once Eichmann was removed from Argentina. Initially, the idea was to return him to Germany, but it was decided at the highest levels of Israeli government to try him in Israel—if he could be captured.

Eichmann Is Brought to Israel and to Justice

Some kind of an excuse was necessary, and finally presented itself in the form of Argentina's 150th anniversary, to be celebrated in May 1960. Israel asked if a delegation headed by Minister of State Abba Eban could attend in order to improve relations between Israel and Argentina. When permission was granted, El Al Airline's New York station manager, Joseph Klein, himself a concentration camp survivor, flew to Buenos Aires to arrange for the landing of a special El Al flight carrying the delegation.

On May 11, Eichmann got off a bus and was walking home from work along General Paz Avenue when an automobile suddenly pulled to the curb and several men jumped out, grabbed him, and threw him into the back seat. It all happened so quickly and quietly that bystanders scarcely realized what had taken place. It turned out later that the abductors were part of a five-man unit of Israeli military commandos led by Yehudah Shimoni.

Eichmann was taken to a safe house, where he underwent a physical examination. He had the scar of an appendectomy, a scar above his left eyebrow, and an SS blood-group tattoo under his left armpit—all matching the German medical records. But the physical examination was only a confirmation: in their first interrogation of their captive, the Israeli commandos had asked his name, "I am Adolf Eichmann," was his prompt reply. "Are you Israelis?"

On May 20, the plane carrying the Israeli delegation landed in Buenos Aires. Within hours it had been refueled and had taken off again, with a reported destination of Rome. (The delegation was stranded, and another plane had to return a week later to pick them up.) Israel has never admitted that Eichmann was taken out on the first plane. In fact, he had been drugged and the Israelis had brought him aboard the plane in a wheelchair. They showed Argentine customs officials an Israeli passport and said that he was a wealthy Jew, near death, who wanted to die in the Promised Land; he was using the unscheduled flight to return there quickly.

Until June 6 Argentina protested continuously over the kidnaping of Eichmann from within its borders. Other nations were sympathetic to Israel's desire to try Eichmann, but, critical of its violation of Argentine jurisdiction. But perhaps the most bizarre story came out on June 6, when the Israelis told Argentina that Eichmann had left "voluntarily" to stand trial in Israel.

Foreign Minister Diogenes Taboada of Argentina released a note in which the Israeli government stated
that Eichmann had been located by a "volunteer"
group in Argentina, where he was living under a false
name without the knowledge of Argentine authorities,
and with the help of other Nazis. The message claimed
that the volunteer group had approached Eichmann
and asked whether he were willing to go to Israel to
stand trial, upon which he asked for twenty-four hours
and then agreed to go. According to the Israeli government, the volunteers then informed their foreign office

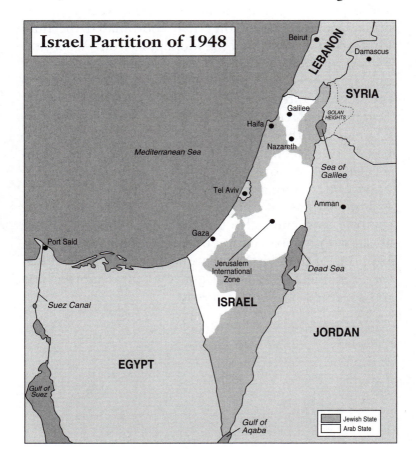

Israel Partition of 1948

Beirut

LEBANON

Damascus

SYRIA

Galilee

GOLAN
HEIGHTS

Haifa

Nazareth

Mediterranean Sea

Sea of
Galilee

Tel Aviv

Amman

Gaza

Port Said

Jerusalem
International
Zone

Dead Sea

Suez Canal

ISRAEL

JORDAN

EGYPT

Gulf of
Suez

Gulf of
Aqaba

Jewish State
Arab State

that Eichmann was in Israel and prepared to face a court. The Israelis expressed regret for the infringement of Argentine sovereignty, but urged consideration of the fact that the man involved had been responsible for the killing of millions of Jews and others. They claimed that members of the volunteer group were survivors of the Nazi massacre of the Jews and that the Israeli government was certain that "the Argentine government will show understanding in the face of such historic and moral values."

After the initial charade of the "independent hunt" and capture of Adolf Eichmann, Israeli secret service officials admitted that they had coordinated the hunt for years and controlled the kidnaping from Argentina. This infuriated the Argentine government, which not only demanded the return of Eichmann, but called on the U.N. [United Nations] for assistance. On June 15, Argentina lodged a formal complaint with the Security Council that the "illicit transfer of Adolf Eichmann to Israel from Argentina had created an atmosphere of insecurity and mistrust incompatible with the preservation of international laws."

The nations of the world knew there would be rhetoric, and knew also that Israel was going to move ahead with its prosecution of Adolf Eichmann.

In one of the most controversial trials in judicial history Eichmann was found guilty of mass murder and was executed on May 31, 1961.

Klaus Barbie: The Butcher of Lyons

UXL

Klaus Barbie's first exposure to the Nazi Party was in 1934 at a voluntary work camp in Schleswig-Holstein. The Nazi precepts taught at the camp intrigued the unemployed twenty-one-year-old and changed him into a full-fledged supporter of Hitler and his Third Reich. One year later, Barbie joined the SS (Schutzstaffel), the protection squad for high-ranking Nazis, later the chief policing agency throughout Germany. By 1940 he had been promoted to *Obersturmfuhrer* (first lieutenant) of the SS in Holland. Later, his promotion to head of the Gestapo in Lyons provided an outlet for his brutality. His ruthless pursuit of Jews and French resistance fighters earned him the notorious title "the Butcher of Lyons." He is credited with the torture and death of Jean Moulin, a leader of the French resistance movement. Hitler awarded Barbie the First Class Iron Cross with Swords for murdering Moulin. After the war, it is believed that Barbie's anti-Communist leanings earned him the protection of American intelligence agents. Living under the alias Klaus Altmann, Barbie obtained Bolivian citizenship in 1957 and remained under the protection of the Bolivian government until 1983, when he was deported to France. Having been tried in absentia twice and sentenced to death for his war crimes, Barbie, at the age of seventy-three, was tried in Lyons. He was convicted

UXL, "Klaus Barbie," *People of the Holocaust*. Farmington Hills, MI: Thomson Gale, 1998. Copyright © 1998 by Thomson Gale. Reproduced by permission.

on 341 counts of crimes against humanity, including murder, extermination, and acts against civilians. He was sentenced to life in prison, where he died in 1991. The following selection describes Barbie's early life, his activities in the SS, his escape to South America, and his eventual arrest and trial. UXL publishes reference materials including encyclopedias, biographies, and almanacs.

🐝   🐝   🐝

Nikolaus (called Klaus) Barbie was born in 1913, the first of two sons born to Nikolaus Barbie and Anna Hees. Both his parents were Catholics and schoolteachers descended from farming families. The couple married when Klaus was three months old.

Nikolaus Senior was badly wounded in World War I (1914–18) when Barbie was just an infant. Although he did not die from the wound until 1933, it caused him so much pain that he took to drinking heavily for relief. When he was drinking, he was often physically abusive to his sons. It is quite possible that young Barbie developed a lifelong hatred for the French because his father had been wounded in the war against them.

Barbie attended the same school where his father taught until he was 11 years old. From 1923 to 1925, he attended boarding school and greatly enjoyed the independence of that experience. For recreation he favored swimming and fencing. In 1925, his family moved to the city of Trier, where Barbie attended secondary school. He was disappointed at having to once again live with his family in their unhappy home. His teachers found him to be an intelligent boy who avoided conflicts. He may have felt drawn to the priesthood at a young age, but this ambition eventually died. He did not pass his school exams until 1934, when he was 20 years old. A year earlier, both his father and brother had died and there was no money for Barbie to attend college. Instead, he volunteered for a work camp run by the National Socialist German Workers' Party (Nazi for short), the political organization headed by Adolf Hitler, who had just risen to power.

Hitler hated the Jews. He believed that they had caused Germany's defeat in World War I. He also believed that they were a "poisonous" race that did not deserve to live. His ultimate goal was to eliminate all the Jews of Europe. Many of the Nazi Party members agreed with Hitler's feelings toward the Jews and were willing to carry out the means to the Jews' destruction.

Barbie Joins the SS

In 1935, not yet 22 years old, Barbie joined the SS, the abbreviation for Schutzstaffel or Security Squad. The unit was originally formed to act as bodyguards for Hitler. In *Klaus Barbie: The Untold Story*, a German newspaperman was quoted by author Ladislas de Hoyos as saying, "All the SS men have this in common: cold eyes like those of fish, reflecting a complete absence of inner life, a complete lack of sentiments." Barbie became a dedicated follower of Hitler. He was an ambitious man whose ultimate goal was the SD, which stands for *Sicherdienst* or Security Police. The SD served as the intelligence (spy) service of the SS. Barbie began a slow but steady rise through the SS ranks. He attended a spy school set up by the Nazis and became an enthusiastic persecutor of Jews in Berlin, Germany's capital city.

Sometime in the late 1930s, Barbie became engaged to Regine Willms, a loyal Nazi Party member who was employed in a Nazi Women's Association nursery school. She was an accomplished cook who liked painting and music. The couple had to pass complicated medical tests devised by SS Chief Heinrich Himmler to make sure they were "racially pure," meaning they had no Jewish blood. After a thorough investigation of his background, Barbie passed the tests; it was noted he had been born the "perfect SS baby." In April 1940, Regine promised to attend the Nazi School for Mothers, in which she would learn to raise children obedient to the Nazis. That month, the couple was finally allowed to marry, eight months after World War II began.

A Cold, Cruel Man

Almost immediately after his wedding ceremony, Barbie was called to active military duty and sent to Amsterdam, Holland. There his primary task was to round up and torment Jews and to keep an eye on Jewish and Christian groups to make sure there was no resistance to Nazi Party policies. Witnesses in Amsterdam later remembered Barbie for his coldness and cruelty. He soon fell out of favor with his supervisor, who complained of Barbie's overfondness for wine and women. He was sent to fight in the Soviet Union (Russia) and then transferred to France in mid-1942. It was in France that his brutality reached its peak.

Because of his training in espionage (spying), Barbie was given the assignment of hunting down leaders of the French resistance, who were French patriots acting secretly to weaken Germany's army in France. Barbie was especially interested in Jean Moulin, who was known to be the right-hand man of French resistance leader Charles de Gaulle. Because French resistance efforts centered around the city of Lyons, Barbie went there to capture Moulin.

While ordinary citizens in Lyons were living on rationed food, SS officers lived like kings. Barbie and other Nazis took over a large hotel and began their activities of arresting, interrogating, beating, and torturing suspected resistance leaders and Jews. Finally, so many people had been placed under arrest that the SS had to move into larger quarters, where an underground network of cellars and thick-walled rooms muffled the screams of SS victims. When Barbie could not convince his prisoners to talk, he kidnapped their family members and threatened to kill them. He was said to be especially fond of kicking and hitting his victims. Sometimes, he let his dogs attack them.

Magnus Linklater and his coauthors offered this portrait of Barbie in *The Nazi Legacy: Klaus Barbie and the International Fascist Connection:* he "considered himself a civilized German: he played the piano, though badly, and enjoyed long . . . discussions about German history and the consequences of the war. He prided himself on his knowledge of France and the French language, and he felt at home in the city of Lyons. He particularly enjoyed his daily walks . . . with his Alsatian, Wolf. . . . Without [his wife], who was for most of the war in [the German city of] Trier, he behaved much like any other unattached officer, eating out in expensive restaurants, getting drunk, and frequenting the nightclubs."

In February 1943, under Barbie's command, a raid was carried out against the offices of a local Jewish organization. Eighty-four people were seized and sent to a concentration camp, where the Nazis confined people they regarded as "enemies of the state." Only 2 of the 84 survived. One of the most hideous crimes Barbie was said to have committed occurred in April 1944; Barbie was later to deny responsibility for the act. It involved a raid carried out on a Jewish children's home in the town of Izeu, in which 43 children aged 3 to 14 years and ten Jewish workers were rounded up and sent to concentration camps. All of the children and nine of the ten workers died in the camps.

Barbie clinched his reputation as "The Butcher of Lyons" with his torture and murder of Jean Moulin, who was the highest-ranking member of the French Resistance ever captured by the Nazis. Moulin was known throughout France as a hero for his bravery in defying the Germans. Barbie, who admired Moulin's courage, considered his capture to be a great personal challenge. In 1943, with the assistance of some French men who betrayed their own leader, Barbie captured Moulin and personally conducted the interview with him.

Despite beatings and torture, Moulin refused to reveal the names of his comrades. Barbie had hoped that his handling of Moulin would ensure a promotion, but he went too far in his "interrogation." On the way to Berlin for further questioning, Moulin died. Barbie later claimed Moulin had killed himself by hurling himself "with incredible violence, head first, against the wall."

In spite of his superiors' disapproval over Moulin's death, Barbie received a medal and was recommended for promotion for his "cleaning out of numerous enemy organizations." But Barbie, himself, was unhappy with his handling of the Moulin affair, and he became moody and unpredictable. He often flew into rages, and his conduct toward prisoners was unspeakably brutal. He began going out into the countryside on surprise raids, rounding up prisoners for questioning. On their way to carry out such a raid in August 1944, Barbie and his men were ambushed, and he suffered several gunshot wounds. He was taken back to Germany and hospitalized.

Barbie just missed the liberation of Paris, France, from the Germans that took place on August 25, 1944. Allied soldiers entered the French capital in a victory that was celebrated around the world. (The Allies were the United States, Great Britain, the Soviet Union, and France.) While Barbie was recovering in the hospital, Germany suffered several more defeats in battle and finally surrendered in May 1945. The war in Europe was over. Barbie was released from the hospital shortly after the surrender, and he was soon rounded up by victorious U.S. troops. In the chaos that surrounded the end of the war, however, Barbie convinced the Americans that he was a French "displaced person." He was given a bicycle and pedaled away.

Postwar Activities

Although there was a warrant out for his arrest, Barbie was able to hide himself from the Allies until 1947. By then, the Allies had found a new enemy—the Soviet Union (Russia) and its economic and social system called communism. Communism aimed for a classless society and was considered a graver threat to world peace than the now-defeated Germans.

The Allies decided they were willing to overlook the crimes of former Nazi leaders to take advantage of their knowledge and skills against the new threat of the Soviet Union. Barbie, still in Germany, was hired as a spy for the United States. Soon he had recruited many of his former Nazi comrades and was running a vast spy ring on the U.S. payroll.

In 1949, Barbie's continued presence in Europe became known to the French, who demanded that he be turned over to them for trial for war crimes (violation of the laws and customs of war). The United States, wishing to conceal the extent of Barbie's secret work for them, arranged for Barbie to escape to South America. He was given false identity papers under the name of Klaus Altmann, which he chose himself. He had known a man by the name of Altmann in the city of Trier, a Jew who later died in the gas chamber at Auschwitz. (A gas chamber is a sealed room that was filled with poisonous gas in order to kill the people locked inside.) In March 1951, the "Altmann family"—Klaus, Regine, their daughter Ute Marie, age nine, and their son Jorge, age four—set sail on an Italian ship for Buenos Aires, Argentina. From Argentina the family soon moved to Bolivia, where Barbie supported himself as an auto mechanic, having been given a quick training course by the American Counter Intelligence Corps (CIC).

But Barbie had too many other "talents" to be satisfied working as a mechanic. South America was a continent at war, and Barbie knew well the ins and outs of war. It was not long before he was involved in theft, fraud, forgery, drug running, arms selling, spying, and politics. He was able to live in luxury once again. He was befriended by Bolivia's president and carried out spy work for him. Barbie also obliged his new friend by training his soldiers in the art of torturing prisoners. All the while he was living openly, dining out in restaurants, and hobnobbing with fellow German exiles.

Finally, in 1971, someone grew suspicious of this German who held Bolivian citizenship and got in touch with the Nazi-hunter Simon Wiesenthal. But it was Nazi-hunter Beate Klarsfeld who actually made the case by identifying "Klaus Altmann" as the notorious "Butcher of Lyons." It was to be twelve years before Barbie was finally brought to justice. In 1983, with a new government in place in Bolivia, Barbie was expelled and sent to France. He was 69 years old and in poor health. He kept insisting that what he had done was "my duty."

The Trial in France

Barbie's return to France for trial caused a sensation. The French were still trying to come to terms with the fact that the Nazis had been aided by thousands of French men and women who were collaborators, people who had turned their own friends, families, and neighbors over to Nazis.

The ailing Barbie sat in jail for four years before his case finally came to trial. Showing no signs of remorse,

Barbie claimed to have no knowledge of what had happened to the Jews he had rounded up and deported (forcibly removed from a city or country). Witnesses testified that he most certainly did know. A telegram he had sent announcing the murder of the children of Izeu was also used as evidence against him.

Finally, on July 4, 1987, Klaus Barbie was found guilty of crimes against humanity and was sentenced to life imprisonment. In 1990, he sought to be released from prison because he had cancer of the blood; his request was refused. He died in prison in 1991. While his victims saw his trial and imprisonment as simple justice, others have asked whether any point was served in bringing this old, sick man—who said he was only following orders—back to France to stand trial.

Appendix of Documents

Document 1: The Twenty-Five Points of the Nazi Party Program

Adolf Hitler and German Workers' Party (DAP) co-founder Anton Drexler wrote these "Twenty-Five Points" and delivered them at a DAP meeting in 1920. The Twenty-Five Points became the foundation of the organization, which would soon officially change its name to the Nazi Party.

The Party Program of the NSDAP was proclaimed on the 24 February 1920 by Adolf Hitler at the first large Party gathering in Munich and since that day has remained unaltered. Within the national socialist philosophy is summarized in 25 points:

1. We demand the unification of all Germans in the Greater Germany on the basis of the right of self-determination of peoples.

2. We demand equality of rights for the German people in respect to the other nations; abrogation of the peace treaties of Versailles and St. Germain.

3. We demand land and territory (colonies) for the sustenance of our people, and colonization for our surplus population.

4. Only a member of the race can be a citizen. A member of the race can only be one who is of German blood, without consideration of creed. Consequently no Jew can be a member of the race.

5. Whoever has no citizenship is to be able to live in Germany only as a guest, and must be under the authority of legislation for foreigners.

6. The right to determine matters concerning administra-

tion and law belongs only to the citizen. Therefore we demand that every public office, of any sort whatsoever, whether in the Reich, the county or municipality, be filled only by citizens. We combat the corrupting parliamentary economy, office-holding only according to party inclinations without consideration of character or abilities.

7. We demand that the state be charged first with providing the opportunity for a livelihood and way of life for the citizens. If it is impossible to sustain the total population of the State, then the members of foreign nations (non-citizens) are to be expelled from the Reich.

8. Any further immigration of non-citizens is to be prevented. We demand that all non-Germans, who have immigrated to Germany since the 2 August 1914, be forced immediately to leave the Reich.

9. All citizens must have equal rights and obligations.

10. The first obligation of every citizen must be to work both spiritually and physically. The activity of individuals is not to counteract the interests of the universality, but must have its result within the framework of the whole for the benefit of all. Consequently we demand:

11. Abolition of unearned (work and labour) incomes. Breaking of rent-slavery.

12. In consideration of the monstrous sacrifice in property and blood that each war demands of the people personal enrichment through a war must be designated as a crime against the people. Therefore we demand the total confiscation of all war profits.

13. We demand the nationalization of all (previous) associated industries (trusts).

14. We demand a division of profits of all heavy industries.

15. We demand an expansion on a large scale of old age welfare.

16. We demand the creation of a healthy middle class and its conservation, immediate communalization of the great warehouses and their being leased at low cost to small firms, the utmost consideration of all small firms in contracts with the State, county or municipality.

17. We demand a land reform suitable to our needs, pro-

vision of a law for the free expropriation of land for the purposes of public utility, abolition of taxes on land and prevention of all speculation in land.

18. We demand struggle without consideration against those whose activity is injurious to the general interest. Common national criminals, usurers, . . . and so forth are to be punished with death, without consideration of confession or race.

19. We demand substitution of a German common law in place of the Roman Law serving a materialistic world-order.

20. The state is to be responsible for a fundamental reconstruction of our whole national education program, to enable every capable and industrious German to obtain higher education and subsequently introduction into leading positions. The plans of instruction of all educational institutions are to conform with the experiences of practical life. The comprehension of the concept of the State must be striven for by the school [Staatsbuergerkunde] as early as the beginning of understanding. We demand the education at the expense of the State of outstanding intellectually gifted children of poor parents without consideration of position or profession.

21. The State is to care for the elevating national health by protecting the mother and child, by outlawing child-labor, by the encouragement of physical fitness, by means of the legal establishment of a gymnastic and sport obligation, by the utmost support of all organizations concerned with the physical instruction of the young.

22. We demand abolition of the mercenary troops and formation of a national army.

23. We demand legal opposition to known lies and their promulgation through the press. In order to enable the provision of a German press, we demand, that: a. All writers and employees of the newspapers appearing in the German language be members of the race; b. Non-German newspapers be required to have the express permission of the State to be published. They may not be printed in the German language; c. Non-Germans are forbidden by law any financial interest in German publications, or any influence on them, and as punishment for violations the closing of such a publi-

cation as well as the immediate expulsion from the Reich of the non-German concerned. Publications which are counter to the general good are to be forbidden. We demand legal prosecution of artistic and literary forms which exert a destructive influence on our national life, and the closure of organizations opposing the above made demands.

24. We demand freedom of religion for all religious denominations within the state so long as they do not endanger its existence or oppose the moral senses of the Germanic race. The Party as such advocates the standpoint of a positive Christianity without binding itself confessionally to any one denomination. It combats the Jewish-materialistic spirit within and around us, and is convinced that a lasting recovery of our nation can only succeed from within on the framework: common utility precedes individual utility.

25. For the execution of all of this we demand the formation of a strong central power in the Reich. Unlimited authority of the central parliament over the whole Reich and its organizations in general. The forming of state and profession chambers for the execution of the laws made by the Reich within the various states of the confederation. The leaders of the Party promise, if necessary by sacrificing their own lives, to support by the execution of the points set forth above without consideration.

Adolf Hitler proclaimed the following explanation for this program on the 13 April 1928:

Explanation

Regarding the false interpretations of Point 17 of the program of the NSDAP on the part of our opponents, the following definition is necessary:

> Since the NSDAP stands on the platform of private ownership it happens that the passage "free expropriation" concerns only the creation of legal opportunities to expropriate if necessary, land which has been illegally acquired or is not administered from the view-point of the national welfare. This is directed primarily against the Jewish land-speculation companies.

The Program of the NSDAP, February 24, 1920.

Document 2: Being True to Hitler's Spirit

Rudolf Hess, Hitler's deputy, made a radio-broadcasted speech on February 24, 1934, in which he administered the Nazi Oath to one million Nazi Party officials across Germany.

German men, German women, German boys, German girls, over a million of you are gathered in many places in all of Germany!

On this the anniversary of the proclamation of the Party's program, you will together swear an oath of loyalty and obedience to Adolf Hitler. You will display to the world what has long been obvious to you, and what you have expressed in past years, often unconsciously. . . .

Being true to Hitler's spirit means knowing that a leader has not only rights, but above all duties. Being true to Hitler's spirit means always being an model. "To be a leader is to be an example," just as Hitler and his work are an example for you. Being true to Hitler's spirit means being modest and unassuming. Being true to Hitler's spirit means remaining a thorough National Socialist in good times and bad. Being a thorough National Socialist means to think ever and only on the whole National Socialist German people. It means that no matter what, always to be a servant of the total National Socialism of Adolf Hitler, to be a fully conscious, heartfelt follower of the Führer above all else. . . .

Your oath is not a mere formality; you do not swear this oath to someone unknown to you. You do not swear in hope, but with certainty. Fate has made it easy for you to take this oath without condition or reservation. Never in history has a people taken an oath to a leader with such absolute confidence as the German people have in Adolf Hitler. You have the enormous joy of taking an oath to a man who is the embodiment of a leader. You take an oath to the fighter who demonstrated his leadership over a decade, who always acts correctly and who always chose the right way, even when at times the larger part of his movement failed to understand why.

You take an oath to a man whom you know follows the laws of providence, which he obeys independently of the influence of earthly powers, who leads the German people rightly, and who will guide Germany's fate. Through your oath you bind yourselves to a man who—that is our faith—was sent to us by higher powers. Do not seek Adolf Hitler with your mind. You will find him through the strength of your hearts!

Adolf Hitler is Germany and Germany is Adolf Hitler. He who takes an oath to Hitler takes an oath to Germany!

Swear to great Germany, to whose sons and daughters throughout the world I send our best wishes.

Rudolf Hess, speech delivered on February 25, 1934.

Document 3: Law for the Protection of German Blood and German Honor

One of the Nuremberg Laws of 1935, the Law for the Protection of German Blood and German Honor forbade marriage between Jews and non-Jews.

Thoroughly convinced by the knowledge that the purity of German blood is essential for the further existence of the German people and animated by the inflexible will to safeguard the German nation for the entire future, the Reichstag has resolved upon the following law unanimously, which is promulgated herewith:

SECTION 1

1. Marriages between Jews and nationals of German or kindred blood are forbidden. Marriages concluded in defiance of this law are void, even if, for the purpose of evading this law, they are concluded abroad.

2. Proceedings for annulment may be initiated only by the Public Prosecutor.

SECTION 2

Relation outside marriage between Jews and nationals for German or kindred blood are forbidden.

SECTION 3

Jews will not be permitted to employ female nationals of German or kindred blood in their households.

SECTION 4

1. Jews are forbidden to hoist the Reich and national flag and to present the colors of the Reich.

2. On the other hand they are permitted to present the Jewish colors. The exercise of this authority is protected by the State.

SECTION 5

1. A person who acts contrary to the prohibition of section 1 will be punished with hard labor.

2. A person who acts contrary to the prohibition of section 2 will be punished with imprisonment or with hard labor.

3. A person who acts contrary to the provisions of section 3 or 4 will be punished with imprisonment up to a year and with a fine or with one of these penalties.

SECTION 6

The Reich Minister of the Interior in agreement with the Deputy of the Fuehrer will issue the legal and administrative regulations which are required for the implementation and supplementation of this law.

SECTION 7

The law will become effective on the day after the promulgation, section 3 however only on 1 January, 1936.

Law for the Protection of German Blood and German Honor, September 15, 1935.

Document 4: With Fire and Sword

The weekly newspaper for SS members calls for the destruction of Jewry in Germany.

We shall now bring the Jewish problem to its complete solution, because it is essential, because we will no longer listen to the outcry in the world, and because actually there is no longer any force in the world that can prevent us from doing so. The plan is clear: total removal, total separation!

What does this mean?

This means not only the removal of the Jews from the economy of the German people, which they damage by their murderous attacks and their incitement to war and to murder.

It means more than that!

No German should be asked to live under the same roof with Jews, who are a race marked as murderers and criminals, and who are the mortal enemies of the German people.

Therefore, we must expel the Jews from our houses and our living areas and house them in separate blocks or streets, where they will live among themselves with as little contact with Germans as possible. They should be marked by a special outward mark, and they should be forbidden to own houses or land, or be partners in any such ownership in Germany. Because it is out of the question to demand of any German that he should be under the authority of a Jewish landowner and that he should keep him by his work. . . .

To criminality.

But let nobody imagine that we can view such a development with equanimity. The German people have no wish to suffer in their midst hundreds of thousands of criminals, who not only maintain themselves by their crime but will also want to take revenge. . . . We would be faced with the hard necessity of exterminating the Jewish underworld in the way we generally exterminate crime in our well-ordered state: with fire and sword. The result would be the actual and final end of Jewry in Germany, its complete destruction.

Das Schwarz Korps, "Jews, What Now?" SS journal, November 24, 1938.

Document 5: A Glorious Page in Our History

On October 4, 1943, Heinrich Himmler, head of the SS, gave a three-hour "moral boosting" speech to SS officers in Posen (also known as Poznan), a city that now lies in Poland, in which he defends the mass killing of Jews.

I also want to talk to you quite frankly about a very grave matter. We can talk about it quite frankly among ourselves and *yet we will never speak of it publicly*. Just as we did not hesitate on 30 June 1934 [the massacre of SA leader Ernst Roehm and other SA commanders] to do our duty as we were bidden, and to stand comrades who had lapsed up against the wall and shoot them, so we have never spoken about it and will never speak of it. It was that tact which is a matter of course, and which I am glad to say is inherent in us, that made us never discuss it among ourselves, never speak of it. It appalled everyone, and yet every [man] was certain that he would do it the next time if such orders should be issued and it should be necessary.

I am referring to the Jewish evacuation programme, *the extermination of the Jewish people*. It is one of those things which are easy to talk about. "The Jewish people will be exterminated", says every party comrade, "It's clear, it's in our programme. Elimination of the Jews, extermination and we'll do it." And then they come along, the worthy eighty million Germans, and each one of them produces his decent Jew. It's clear the others are swine, but this one is a fine Jew. Not one of those who talk like that has watched it happening, not one of them has been through it. *Most of you will know what it means when a hundred corpses are lying side by side, or five hundred or a thousand are lying there. To have stuck it out and—apart from a few exceptions due to human weakness—to have remained decent, that is what has made us tough.* This is a glorious page in our history, and one that has never been written and can never be written. For we know how difficult we would have made it for ourselves if, on top of the bombing raids, the burdens and deprivations of war, we still had Jews today in every town as secret saboteurs, agitators and troublemakers. We would now probably have reached the 1916–17 stage when the Jews were still part of the body of the German nation.

We have taken from them what wealth they had. I have issued a strict order . . . that this wealth should, as a matter of course, be handed over to the Reich without reserve. We have taken none of it for ourselves. Individual men who have lapsed will be punished in accordance with an order I issued at the beginning which gave this warning: Whoever takes so much as a mark of it is a dead man. A number of SS men—there are not very many of them—have fallen short, and they will die, without mercy. We had the moral right, we had the duty to our people, to destroy this people which wanted to destroy us. But we have not the right to enrich ourselves with so much as a fur, a watch, a mark, a cigarette or anything else. We have exterminated a bacterium because we do not want in the end to be infected by the bacterium and die of it. I will not see so much as a small area of sepsis appear here or gain a hold. Wherever it may form, we will cauterize it. All in all, we can say that we fulfilled this most difficult duty for the love of our people. *And our spirit, our soul, our character has not suffered injury from it.* (emphasis added)

Heinrich Himmler, speech given to SS leaders, October 4, 1943.

Document 6: Hitler's Sportspalast Speech

On September 26, 1938, Hitler gave his famous Sportspalast speech in which he stated that if the Sudeten territories were forfeited by Czechoslovakia, Germany would seek no further territorial conquests.

I have attacked all seemingly impossible problems with a firm will to solve them peaceably if at all feasible even at the risk of more or less important German sacrifices. . . .

Now we confront the last problem that must and shall be solved.

This is the last territorial demand I have to make in Europe, but it is a demand on which I will not yield.

Its history is as follows: In 1918 Central Europe was torn up and reshaped by some foolish or crazy so-called statesmen under the slogan "self-determination and the right of nations."

Without regard to history, origin of peoples, their national wishes, their economic necessities, they smashed up Europe and arbitrarily set up new States.

To this, Czechoslovakia owed its existence.

This Czech State began with one big lie and its father's name was [Eduard] Benes [Czechoslovakian president].

This Herr Benes at that time turned up at Versailles and told them that there was the Czechoslovak nation.

He had to invent this lie to bolster up an insignificant number of his own nationals so as to make them seem more important.

I said in the Reichstag on Feb. 20, that this must be changed. Only Herr Benes changed it differently. He started a more radical system of oppression, greater terror, a period of dissolutions, bans, confiscations, etc.

This went on until May 21, and you cannot deny, my friends, that it was truly endless German patience that we practiced.

This May 21 was unbearable enough. I have told the story of this month already at the Reich's party convention.

There at last were to be elections in Czechoslovakia. They could no longer be postponed.

So Herr Benes thinks out a way to intimidate Germans there—military occupation of those sections.

He still keeps up this military occupation in the expectation that so long as his hirelings are there nobody will dare raise a hand against him.

It was an impudent lie that Germany had mobilized. That had to be used in order to cloak the Czech mobilization, excuse it and explain it.

What happened then, you know. The infamous international world set at Germany. Germany had not called upon one man. It never thought of solving this problem militarily.

I still had hopes that the Czechs would recognize at the last minute that this tyrannic regime could not keep up.

But Herr Benes believed Germany was fair game. Of course, he thought he was covered by France and England and nothing could possibly happen to him.

And if everything failed there still was Soviet Russia to fall back on.

Thus the answer of that man was: No, more than ever, shoot down, arrest and incarcerate all those whom he did not like for some reason. Then, finally, my demands came from Nuremberg.

The demands now were quite clear. Now, for the first time, I said, that at last nearly twenty years after Mr. [Woodrow] Wilson's right of self-determination for the 3,500,000 must be enforced and we shall not just look on any longer.

And again Herr Benes replied: New victims, new incarcerations, new arrests. The German element gradually began to flee.

Then came England. I informed Mr. [Nelville] Chamberlain [British prime minister] unequivocally of what we regard as the only possibility of solution.

It is the most natural solution possible.

I know that all these nationalities no longer want to remain with this Herr Benes.

In the first place, however, I speak of Germans. For these Germans I have now spoken and now given assurances that I am no longer willing to look on quietly and passively as this lunatic believes he can simply mishandle 3,500,000 human beings.

I left no doubt that German patience at last was exhausted. I left no doubt it was the way of our German mentality to take things long and patiently, that, however, the moment comes once when this must be ended.

And now, in fact, England and France agreed to dispatch the only possible demand to Czechoslovakia, namely to free the German region and cede it to the Reich.

I am thankful to Mr. Chamberlain for all his trouble and I assured him that the German people wants nothing but peace, but I also declared that I cannot go beyond the limits of our patience.

I further assured him and I repeat here that if this problem is solved, there will be no further territorial problems in Europe for Germany.

And I further assured him that at the moment that Czechoslovakia has solved her other problems, that is, when the Czechs have reconciled themselves with their other minorities, the Czech State no longer interests me and that, if you please, I give him the guarantee: We do not want any Czechs.

But equally I want now to declare before the German people that as regards the Sudeten German problem, my patience is now exhausted.

I now head the procession of my people as first soldier and behind me—may the world know this—there now marches a people and a different one than that of 1918.

Errant mentors of those times succeeded in infiltrating the poison of democratic phrases into our people, but the German people of today is not the German people of 1918.

In these hours we will take one holy common resolve. It shall be stronger than any pressure, any peril. And when this will is stronger than pressure and peril, it will break the pressure and peril.

Adolf Hitler, Sportspalast speech, September 26, 1938.

Document 7: The German People Is No Warlike Nation

Hitler elaborates on Germany's international relations in this speech before the German Reichstag on February 20, 1938.

There are more than ten million Germans in states adjoining Germany which before 1866 were joined to the bulk of the German nation by a national link. Until 1918 they fought in the Great War shoulder to shoulder with the German soldiers of the Reich. Against their own free will they were prevented by peace treaties from uniting with the Reich.

This was painful enough, but there must be no doubt about one thing: political separation from the Reich may not lead to deprivation of rights, that is the general rights of racial self-determination which were solemnly promised to us in [U.S. president Woodrow] Wilson's Fourteen Points as a condition for the armistice. We cannot disregard it just because this is a case concerning Germans.

In the long run it is unbearable for a world power, conscious of herself, to know there are citizens at her side who are constantly being inflicted with the severest sufferings for their sympathy or unity with the total nation, its faith and philosophy.

We will know there can scarcely be a frontier line in Europe which satisfies all. It should be all the more important to avoid the torture of national minorities in order not to add to the suffering of political separation, the suffering of persecution on account of their belonging to a certain people.

That it is possible to find ways leading to the lessening of tension has been proved. But he who tries to prevent by force such lessening of tension through creating an equilibrium in Europe will someday inevitably conjure up force among the nations themselves. It cannot be denied that Germany herself, as long as she was powerless and defenseless, was compelled to tolerate many of these continual persecutions of the German people on our frontier.

But just as England stands up for her interests all over the globe, present-day Germany will know how to guard its more restricted interests. To these interests of the German Reich belong also the protection of those German peoples who are not in a position to secure along our frontiers their political and philosophical freedom by their own efforts.

I may say that since the League of Nations has abandoned its continuous attempts at disturbance in Danzig and since the advent of the new commissioner this most dangerous place for European peace has entirely lost its menace.

Poland respects the national conditions in the free city of Danzig and Germany respects Polish rights.

Now I turn to Austria. It is not only the same people but above all a long communal history and culture which bind together the Reich and Austria.

Difficulties which emerged in the carrying out of the agreement of July 11, 1936, made essential an attempt to remove misunderstandings and obstacles to final reconciliation. It is clear that whether we wished it or not an intolerable position might have developed that would have contained the seeds of catastrophe. It does not lie in the power of man to stop the rolling stone of fate which through neglect or lack of wisdom has been set moving.

I am happy to say that these ideas correspond with the viewpoint of the Austrian chancellor, whom I invited to visit me. The underlying intention was to bring about a détente in our relations which would guarantee to National Socialist sympathizers in Austria within the limits of the law the same rights enjoyed by other citizens.

In connection with it there was to be an act of conciliation in the form of a general amnesty and better understanding between the two states through closer and friendlier relations in the various spheres of cultural, political, and economic cooperation. All this is a development within the framework of the treaty of July 11.

I wish to pay tribute to the Austrian chancellor for his efforts to find together with me a way which is just as much in the interests of both countries as in that of the entire German people, whose sons we all are regardless of where we came from. I believe we have thus made a contribution to European peace.

Our satisfactory relations with other countries are known

to all. Above all is to be mentioned our cooperation with those two great powers which, like Germany, have recognized bolshevism as a world danger and are therefore determined to resist the Comintern with a common defense. It is my earnest wish to see this cooperation with Italy and Japan more and more extended.

The German people is no warlike nation. It is a soldierly one which means it does not want a war but does not fear it. It loves peace, but it also loves its honor and freedom.

The new Reich shall belong to no class, no profession, but to the German poeple. It shall help the people find an easier road in this world. It shall help them in making their lot a happier one. Party, state, armed forces, economics are institutions and functions which can only be estimated as a means toward an end. They will be judged by history according to the services they render toward this goal. Their purpose, however, is to serve the people.

I now pray to God that he will bless in the years to come our work, our deeds, our foresight, our resolve; that the almighty may protect us from both arrogance and cowardly servility, that he may help us find the right way which he has laid down for the German people and that he may always give us courage to do the right thing and never to falter or weaken before any power or any danger.

Long live Germany and the German people!

Adolf Hitler, speech before the German Reichstag, February 20, 1938.

Document 8: Interrogation of Adolf Eichmann

After being captured in Buenos Aires, Adolf Eichmann, who implemented the Final Solution, was brought to Israel in 1960. During his interrogation prior to his trial, he gave his version of Nazi atrocities and the role he played in them.

[Captain Avner Less, interrogator] You keep trying to convince me that in Reich territory it was the Gauleiters who pressed to have the Jews in their Gaus evacuated as quickly as possible. I'm going to read from the minutes of a meeting: "Gauleiters or Kreisleiters are to be informed of the evacuations, because several Gauleiters complained that they have received no notice of such crucial measures."

EICHMANN: Naturally, with so many actions under way, the local evacuation authorities didn't always observe the guidelines. The bureau never took it on itself to say: Look here. There are still . . . two thousand or five thousand Jews here . . . in, say . . . Rhineland-Westphalia, we want to get them out of here, and on the double. That wasn't the province of [Eichmann's] Bureau IV B 4. It never did anything like that, because so many orders were always coming in from the Reichsführer and the head of the Security Police that we were glad if we could just get half enough transportation for those jobs and arrange the routing and scheduling with the Transportation Ministry. We, the bureau I mean, really had no need to make extra work for ourselves. We already had it up to here.

LESS: You keep saying that this, that, and the other thing weren't in your department. There are hundreds and thousands of details which you took an interest in but which were not in your department. If they were not in your department, why do we find time and again, in all these documents, that you did take a hand in them?

EICHMANN: Well, Herr Hauptmann, [Mr. Captain] all those things were inseparably connected with evacuation.

LESS: That's just it. One might say, for instance: no evacuation, no gas chambers.

EICHMANN: Yes . . . you could put it that way . . . though I had nothing to do with that sector.

LESS: You say you had nothing to do with the killing?

EICHMANN: That's right.

LESS: But you delivered the people to be killed.

EICHMANN: Yes, sir, that is true, insofar as I received orders to evacuate them. But not all the people I evacuated were killed. I had no knowledge whatever of who was killed and who was not. Otherwise, 2.4 million Jews would not, according to one count, have been found alive after the war.

LESS: It's no thanks to you that any Jews were found alive after the war. If the war had gone on longer, those two million would in all likelihood have been killed. Your plan called for total extermination of the Jews.

EICHMANN: Not my plan. I had nothing to do with that plan, Herr Hauptmann.

LESS: You certainly had the plan in your possession, because—

EICHMANN: I am obviously guilty of complicity. That is plain. I've said so before. To that extent, Herr Hauptmann, I cannot deny my responsibility, and any attempt to do so would be absurd. Because from a juridical point of view I am guilty of complicity.

LESS: We're not talking about the juridical point of view. We're talking about cold facts.

EICHMANN: Yes, but I mean, on the strength of these cold facts, I am guilty of complicity . . . from the standpoint of jurisprudence. That's obvious. I realize that, and I'm not trying it. . . . I can't try . . . to sidestep . . . to talk myself out of it.

LESS: Very well, but in all your statements you keep hiding behind "it wasn't in my department," "it wasn't in my province," "the regulations" . . .

EICHMANN: Yes, Herr Hauptmann, I have to do that, because as head of Bureau IV B 4 I was really not answerable for everything, but only for my rather narrowly circumscribed department. And this narrowly circumscribed sphere is easily definable, because we were a central office.

Jochen von Lang, ed., *Eichmann Interrogated.* New York: Farrar, Straus & Giroux, 1983, pp. 103–105.

Document 9: Albert Speer Regrets Joining Nazi Party

In this excerpt from his memoirs, Albert Speer, Hitler's architect, berates himself for not knowing what the Nazi Party was planning, and regrets his association with Hitler and the Nazis.

Quite often even the most important step in a man's life, his choice of vocation, is taken quite frivolously. He does not bother to find out enough about the basis and the various aspects of that vocation. Once he has chosen it, he is inclined to switch off his critical awareness and to fit himself wholly into the predetermined career.

My decision to enter Hitler's party was no less frivolous.

Why, for example, was I willing to abide by the almost hypnotic impression Hitler's speech had made upon me? Why did I not undertake a thorough, systematic investigation of, say, the value or worthlessness of the ideologies of *all* the parties? Why did I not read the various party programs, or at least Hitler's *Mein Kampf* and Rosenberg's *Myth of the Twentieth Century*? As an intellectual I might have been expected to collect documentation with the same thoroughness and to examine various points of view with the same lack of bias that I had learned to apply to my preliminary architectural studies. This failure was rooted in my inadequate political schooling. As a result, I remained uncritical, unable to deal with the arguments of my student friends, who were predominantly indoctrinated with the National Socialist ideology.

For had I only wanted to, I could have found out even then that Hitler was proclaiming expansion of the Reich to the east; that he was a rank anti-Semite; that he was committed to a system of authoritarian rule; that after attaining power he intended to eliminate democratic procedures and would thereafter yield only to force. Not to have worked that out for myself; not, given my education, to have read books, magazines, and newspapers of various viewpoints; not to have tried to see through the whole apparatus of mystification—was already criminal. At this initial stage my guilt was as grave as, at the end, my work for Hitler. For being in a position to know and nevertheless shunning knowledge creates direct responsibility for the consequences—from the very beginning. . . .

By entering Hitler's party I had already, in essence, assumed a responsibility that led directly to the brutalities of forced labor, to the destruction of war, and to the deaths of those millions of so-called undesirable stock—to the crushing of justice and the elevation of every evil. In 1931 I had no idea that fourteen years later I would have to answer for a host of crimes to which I subscribed beforehand by entering the party. I did not yet know that I would atone with twenty-one years of my life for frivolity and thoughtlessness and breaking with tradition. Still, I will never be rid of that sin.

Albert Speer, *Inside the Third Reich*. Trans. Richard and Clara Winston. New York: Macmillan, 1970, pp. 21–24.

For Further Research

Biographies of Hitler

Lev Bezymenski, *The Death of Adolf Hitler: Unknown Documents from Soviet Archives*. New York: Harcourt, Brace, and World, 1968.

Allan Bullock, *Hitler: A Study in Tyranny*. New York: Harper and Row, 1971.

Joachim C. Fest, *Hitler*. Trans. Richard and Clara Winston. New York: Harcourt Brace Jovanovich, 1973.

Charles Bracelen Flood, *Hitler: The Path to Power*. New York: Houghton Mifflin, 1989.

Ian Kershaw, *Hitler: 1936–1945, Nemesis*. New York: W.W. Norton, 2000.

Robert Payne, *The Life and Death of Adolf Hitler*. New York: Praeger, 1973.

Ron Rosenbaum, *Explaining Hitler: The Search for the Origins of His Evil*. New York: Random House, 1998.

Biographies of Hitler's Henchmen

Richard Breitman, *The Architect of Genocide: Himmler and the Final Solution*. New York: Alfred A. Knopf, 1991.

Helmut Heiber, *Goebbels*. New York: Hawthorn, 1972.

Ladislas de Hoyos, *Klaus Barbie*. Trans. Nicholas Courtin. New York: McGraw-Hill, 1985.

Harel Isser, *The House on Garibaldi Street: The First Full Account of the Capture of Adolf Eichmann*. New York: Viking, 1975.

Roger Manvell and Heinrich Fraenkel, *Dr. Goebbels: His Life and Death*. New York: Simon & Schuster, 1960.

———, *Goering*. New York: Simon & Schuster, 1962.

Leonard Mosley, *The Reich Marshall: A Biography of Hermann Goering*. Garden City, NY: Doubleday, 1974.

Peter Padfield, *Himmler*. New York: Henry Holt, 1990.

Viktor Reimann, *Goebbels: The Man Who Created Hitler*. Garden City, NY: Doubleday, 1976.

Ralf Georg Reuth, *Goebbels*. New York: Harcourt Brace, 1990.

Wulf Schwarzwaller, *Rudolph Hess: The Last Nazi*. Bethesda, MD: National, 1988.

Bradley F. Smith, *Heinrich Himmler: A Nazi in the Making*. Stanford, CA: Hoover Institution, 1971.

Albert Speer, *Inside the Third Reich*. New York: Macmillan, 1970.

Robert Wistrich, *Who's Who in Nazi Germany*. New York: Routledge, 1995.

Nazi Germany

William Sheridan Allen, *The Nazi Seizure of Power: The Experience of a Single German Town, 1922–1945*. New York: Franklin Watts, 1984.

Willi A. Boelcke, *The Secret Conferences of Dr. Goebbels: The Nazi Propaganda War, 1939–1943*. New York: E.P. Dutton, 1970.

Martin Broszat, *Hitler and the Collapse of Weimer Germany*. Oxford, UK: Berg, 1987.

George C. Browder, *Hitler's Enforcers: The Gestapo and the SS*

Security Services in the Nazi Revolution. New York: Oxford University Press, 1996.

Eugene Davidson, *The Making of Adolf Hitler: The Birth and Rise of Nazism.* Columbia: University of Missouri Press, 1977.

Harold C. Deutsch, *Hitler and His Generals: The Hidden Crisis, January–June 1938.* Minneapolis: University of Minnesota Press, 1974.

E.J. Feuchtwanger, *From Weimer to Hitler: Germany, 1918–1933.* New York: St. Martin's, 1995.

Klaus P. Fischer, *Nazi Germany: A New History.* New York: Continuum, 1995.

Peter Fritzsche, *Germans into Nazis.* Cambridge, MA: Harvard University Press, 1998.

Robert Gellately, *The Gestapo and German Society: Enforcing Racial Policy, 1933–1945.* New York: Oxford University Press, 1990.

Frederick V. Grunfeld, *The Hitler File: A Social History of Germany and the Nazis, 1918–1945.* New York: Random House, 1974.

Michael H. Kater, *The Nazi Party: Social Profile of Members and Leaders, 1919–1945.* Cambridge, MA: Harvard University Press, 1983.

Louis C. Kilzer, *Churchill's Deception: The Dark Secret That Destroyed Nazi Germany.* New York: Simon & Schuster, 1994.

H.W. Koch, *The Hitler Youth: Origins and Development, 1922–1945.* New York: Stein and Day, 1975.

Claudia Koonz, *Mothers in the Fatherland.* New York: St. Martin's, 1988.

Yaacov Lozowick, *Hitler's Bureaucrats: The Nazi Security Police and the Banality of Evil.* Trans. Haim Watzman. New York: Continuum, 2003.

John Lukacs, *The Hitler of History*. New York: Vintage, 1998.

Bruno Manz, *A Mind in Prison: The Memoir of a Son and Soldier of the Third Reich*. Washington, DC: Brassey's, 2000.

Samuel W. Mitcham Jr., *Why Hitler? The Genesis of the Nazi Reich*. Westport, CT: Praeger, 1996.

David Welch, *The Third Reich: Politics and Propaganda*. New York: Routledge, 1995.

Ian Westwell, *In the Path of Hitler's Third Reich: The Journey from Victory to Defeat*. New York: Gramercy, 1998.

The Holocaust

Michael Berenbaum, *The World Must Know: The History of the Holocaust as Told in the United States Holocaust Memorial Museum*. Boston: Little, Brown, 1993.

Martin Gilbert, *The Holocaust: A History of the Jews of Europe During the Second World War*. New York: Holt, Rinehart and Winston, 1985.

——, *Never Again: A History of the Holocaust*. New York: Universe, 2000.

Daniel Jonah Goldhagen, *Hitler's Willing Executioners: Ordinary Germans and the Holocaust*. New York: Alfred A. Knopf, 1996.

Marion A. Kaplan, *Between Dignity and Despair: Jewish Life in Nazi Germany*. New York: Oxford University Press, 1998.

Michael R. Marcus, *The Holocaust in History*. Hanover, NH: University Press of New England, 1987.

Lili Meier, ed., *Auschwitz Album: A Book Based upon an Album Discovered by a Concentration Camp Survivor*. New York: Random House, 1982.

Dalia Ofer and Lenore J. Weitzman, eds., *Women in the Holocaust*. New Haven, CT: Yale University Press, 1998.

Mordecai Paldiel, *Saving the Jews*. Rockville, MD: Schreiber, 2000.

Sylvia Rothchild, ed., *Voices from the Holocaust*. New York: New American Library, 1981.

Web Sites

Gates to Hell: The Nazi Death Camps, www.deathcamps. info. This site gives general information on the death camps, provides answers to frequently asked Holocaust-related questions, and provides sources for further reading about Hitler, his henchmen, and the Holocaust. The author, Louis Bälow, has written for newspapers and magazines on the subjects of World War II and the Holocaust.

The Nizkor Project, www.nizkor.org. Named for the Hebrew word meaning "we will remember," the Nizkor Project Web site contains the largest archive of Holocaust-related documents on the Internet. Includes transcripts of the Nuremberg trial of major German war criminals, Nazi biographies, and statistics on the death camps. Some documents are in Spanish.

Yad Vashem, www.yadvashem.org. This is the site of the fifty-year-old organization that honors both Holocaust martyrs as well as heroes. The site contains pictures of Holocaust artifacts that are part of Yad Vashem's Historical Museum Collection as well as links to a Holocaust research center and an Auschwitz album. The site contains 213 documents in English.

Index

Adolf Hitler Fund, 121
Amen, John, 171
Angriff, Der (newspaper), 68
Anschluss, 191
anti-Semitism
  Goebbels and promotion
    of, 70
  of Hitler, source of, 13, 29,
    201
  Nuremberg Laws and,
    53–55
Arbeitsgemeinschaft der
  Vaterlaendischen
  Kampfverbaende (Working
  Union of the Fatherland
  Fighting Leagues), 38
Ariosophy, 29
Aryans, 12, 29
Ashman, Charles, 189, 190
Auschwitz
  Höss as commandant of,
    169–70
  Höss on, 168–69, 172–74
  Mengele at, 178, 179–83
Austria, 191
  Hitler's intentions for, 56
Axmann, Artur, 128

Bach-Zelewski, Erich von
  dem, 96–97
Barbie, Klaus

early life of, 200–201
  as spy for U.S., 205
  trial of, 206–207
Bauer, Fritz, 193
Beer Hall Putsch
  Göring and, 40–41, 81
  Hess and, 106
  Röhm and, 142, 145–46
Ben-Gurion, David, 192
Bernadotte (Swedish count),
  163
Bird, Eugene K., 110, 112
Blood Order of the NSDAP
  medal, 117
Blood Purge. *See* Night of
  the Long Knives
book burnings, 73–74
Bormann, Martin, 84, 134
  as Hitler's confidant,
    123–25
  during last weeks of war,
    126–27
  as Nazi Party assistant, 118
  offices held by, 115
Brandt, Karl, 136
Braun, Eva, 83
Brown Shirts. *See*
  Sturmabteilung
Brueckner, Wilhelm, 40
Buch (Bormann), Gerda,
  119, 126

Bülow, Bernard von, 156

Chamberlain, Neville, 56
Christianity, Bormann and,
    122–23
Churchill, Winston, 159
Committee of Three, 124
concentration camps. *See*
    extermination camps
Cyclon B gas, 173
Czechoslovakia, Hitler's
    intentions for, 56

Dawidowicz, Lucy S., 52
de Gaulle, Charles, 202
Deutscher Kampfbund
    (German Fighting Union),
    38
Dietrich, Joseph Sepp, 151,
    152
Dietrich, Otto, 111
Dolchstoss (stab-in-the-
    back theory), 59
Dönitz, Karl, 101, 128, 138
    as critic of Ribbentrop,
    156
Drexler, Anton, 14, 34
Dutch, Oswald, 16

Eban, Abba, 195
Eckart, Dietrich, 33–34
Eichmann, Adolf
    as architect of Final
    Solution, 190
    capture of, 195–98
    joins SS, 191
    in South America, 192–95
Eicke, Theodor, 170
Eingruber, August, 133
Eisenhower, Dwight D.,
    138

Ernst, Karl, 150–51
Esser, Hermann, 57, 111
extermination camps
    Höss on, 172
    human experimentation in,
    97–98, 183–84

Face of the Third Reich, The
    (Fest), 14, 90
Faulk, Karin von, 80
Feder, Gottfried, 34
Fest, Joachim C., 14, 90
Final Solution
    Eichmann as architect of,
    190
    planning for
    implementation of, 57–58
    see also Holocaust
Four Year Plan, 55
Fraenkel, Heinrich, 165
France, occupation of Ruhr
    by, 37–38
Freikorps, 143, 145
French resistance, 202
Frick, Wilhelm, 42
Funk, Walther, 111

German-Soviet
    nonaggression pact (1939),
    156
German Workers' Party
    (DAP), 13, 33
Gilbert, Gustav M., 131,
    138–39
    on Höss, 166, 167
Goebbels, Magda, 71
Goebbels, Paul Joseph
    Blood Purge and, 150, 151
    diaries of, 63–64
    on Hitler, 64–65, 66–67
    reveal Goebbels's

attitudes, 65–66
reveal Goebbels's
characteristics, 74–75
joins Nazi Party, 63–64
motives of, 15, 17
rise in power of, 68–69
Göring, Emmy Sonnemann,
81–82
Göring, Hermann, 57, 70
attempts negotiation with
Allies, 162–63
Blood Purge and, 151
characteristics of, 160–62
as critic of Ribbentrop,
159, 160
on Hess, 109
during last weeks of war,
127
motives of, 15, 17–18
as natural leader, 85–86
at Nuremberg trials, 87–89
offices held by, 78
personality of, 77–78
Graf, Ulrich, 41
in Beer Hall Putsch, 48

Hanfstaengl, Ernst (Putzi),
49
Harrer, Karl, 33
Haushofer, Karl, 105
Hees, Anna, 200
Henckel (Ribbentrop),
Annelise, 155, 157–59
Hess, Rudolf, 50, 114, 119,
120
in Beer Hall Putsch, 41, 48
early life of, 104
in Landsberg prison,
106–107
motives of, 17–18
offices held by, 106–107

peace mission of, 108–109
political development of,
104–106
Hess: The Man and His
Mission (Hutton), 110
Heydrich, Reinhard, 57, 93
Himmler, Heinrich, 15,
20–21, 57, 78, 135, 179
Blood Purge and, 151
early life of, 79–80
on Hitler, 99
Hitler is betrayed by,
100–102
during last weeks of war,
127
as most extreme of Hitler's
followers, 95–97
terrorism institutionalized
by, 94–96
utopian fanaticism of,
97–98
Hindenburg, Paul von, 39
Hitler, Adolf
Beer Hall Putsch and,
40–49
Bormann and, 115, 119–21
early life of, 25–26
Goebbels on, 64–65,
66–67
Göring on, 87–88
Himmler on, 99
Himmler's betrayal of,
100–102
invasion plans of, 56
messianic mission of, 59
political agenda of, 11–13
political development of,
28–30, 32–35
Ribbentrop and, 156
Röhm and, 152
fallout between, 146–50

friendship between, 144
Speer becomes
  disillusioned with, 133,
  137
suicide of, 11
treason trial of, 50–51
in Vienna, 26–28, 30–31
in World War I, 31–32
Hitler and Nazi Germany
  (Spielvogel), 24
Hitler and the Nazi Leaders:
  A Unique Insight into Evil
  (Lattimer), 129–30, 153
Hitler's Twelve Apostles
  (Dutch), 16
Hitler: The Pathology of Evil
  (Victor), 19
Hitler Youth, 127
Hoess, Rudolf. *See* Höss,
  Rudolf
Holocaust, 16
  circumstances leading to,
  52, 58–59
  see also Final Solution
Hoover, Herbert, 63
Höss, Rudolf, 102
  early life of, 166–67
  in Freikorps, 167
  at Nuremberg trials,
  171–75
  at Polish tribunal, 175–76
Hossbach protocol, 56
Hoyos, Ladislas de, 201
human experimentation
  Himmler and, 97–98
  Mengele and, 183–84
Hutton, B., 110

Incomparable Crime, The
  (Manvell and Fraenkel),
  165

International Military
  Tribunal at Nuremberg.
  See Nuremberg,
  International Military
  Tribunal at
Israel
  capture of Eichmann by,
  192–93, 195–98
  map of 1948 partition of,
  197

Jackson, Robert H., 138
Jews
  Eichmann and
  resettlement of, 191–92
  Hitler's mission to
  exterminate, 52–59
  see also anti-Semitism
Jodl, Alfred, 83, 111
Journalists' Law, 70

Kahr, Gustav von, 39–40
  in Beer Hall Putsch, 42,
  43, 45, 46
Kaltenbrunner, Ernst, 84,
  163, 191
Kampfbund, 146–47
Kapos, 170
Keitel, Wilhelm, 57, 111,
  124
Kelley, Douglas M., 76, 156
Kersten, Felix, 91, 99
Kesselring, Albert von, 85
Klarsfeld, Beate, 187
Klaus Barbie: The Untold
  Story (Hoyos), 201
Klein, Joseph, 195
Knopp, Guido, 17
Koch, Friedrich, 136
Kristallnacht (Night of
  Broken Glass), 56–57

Goebbels's denial of,
72–73
Kubizek, August, 25, 27, 28

Lammers, Hans, 124
Lang, Jochen von, 114
Langbein, Hermann, 175,
182
Langer, Walter C., 13, 19
Lattimer, John K., 129, 153
Law for the Protection of
German Blood and Honor,
54
Lebensborn eV, 94
Levy, Yedidya, 193
Liebenfels, Lanz von (Adolf
Lanz), 24, 29, 33
Linklater, Magnus, 203
Lochner, Louis P., 61, 62
Lohengrin (Wagner), 30
London Agreement (1945),
10
Lossow, Otto von, 40
in Beer Hall Putsch, 42,
43, 45
Low, Alfred D., 103, 104
Ludendorff, Erich
Beer Hall Putsch and,
43–44, 46
Hitler and, 38–39
treason trial of, 50–51
Lueger, Karl, 24, 28–29
Lutze, Viktor, 150, 151

Manvell, Roger, 165
Mein Kampf (Hitler), 28, 51,
137
on Hitler's messianic
mission, 59
on Hitler's relationship
with German Workers'

Party, 34
is transformed to state
policy, 55
writing of, 106
*Men Around Hitler: The
Nazi Elite and Its
Collaborators, The* (Low),
103
Mengele, Josef
at Auschwitz, 179–83
early life of, 178
medical experiments of,
183–84
postwar escape of, 184–85
search for, 185–88
Miale, Florence, 21
Mind of Hitler, The (Langer),
19
Moulin, Jean, 199, 202,
203–204
Mueller, Karl Alexander
von, 45
Munich Pact, 156
Mussolini, Benito, 37, 125

National Socialist German
Workers' Party (Nazi
Party, NSDAP)
creation of, 14, 35
growth in, 119
National-Sozialistische
Briefe (National Socialist
Letters), 67–68
*Nazi Elite: Shocking Profiles
of the Reich's Most Notorious
Henchmen, The* (Snyder),
177
Nazi Hunters, The (Ashman
and Wagman), 190
*Nazi Legacy: Klaus Barbie
and the International Fascist*

Connection (Linklater et
al.), 203
Nazi Party. *See* National
Socialist German Workers'
Party
Neave, Alrey, 108
Neurath, Konstantin von,
155, 159
New York Times
(newspaper), 192
Night of Broken Glass. *See*
Kristallnacht
Night of the Long Knives,
20, 125, 150–52
Himmler and, 92–93
NSDAP. *See* National
Socialist German Workers'
Party
Nuremberg, International
Military Tribunal at, 10–11
charges against Nazi
leaders at, 115
Göring at, 87–89
Höss at, 171–75
Nuremberg Laws, 53–55
Hess and, 108
*Nuremberg Mind: The
Psychology of the Nazi
Leaders, The* (Miale and
Selzer), 21

ODESSA, 184
Operation Barbarossa, 58

Papen, Franz von, 134
as critic of Ribbentrop,
156, 159
Poland, Hitler's plans for,
57–58
Poznan speech (Himmler),
95, 102

Prisoner #7, Rudolf Hess
(Bird), 110
Prohl (Prönl), Ilse, 18, 106
propaganda, Goebbels and,
69–70

Rath, Ernest vom, 56
Reich Center for Jewish
Emigration, 192
Reich Citizenship Law, 54
Reich Culture Chamber
Law, 70
Reich Ministry for Public
Enlightenment and
Propaganda, 69–70
Reichszentrale, 57
Ribbentrop, Joachim von,
15, 78, 84
diplomatic style of,
159–60
early life of, 154
as family man, 158–59
as foreign minister,
155–58
in WWI, 154–55
Ribbentrop Bureau, 157
Rienzi (Wagner), 30
*Rise and Fall of the Third
Reich, The* (Shirer), 19
Röhm, Ernst, 14–15, 17–18,
94, 142–52
Beer Hall Putsch and, 38,
46
Blood Purge and, 150–52
in Bolivia, 147–48
execution of, 20, 93, 152
fallout between Hitler and,
146–50
in Freikorps, 143
Rosenberg, Alfred, 34, 178,
179

Rossbach Organization, 117
Ruhr, French occupation of,
37–38

Schacht, Hjalmar, 134
as critic of Ribbentrop,
156, 159
Schellenberg, Walter, 99
Scheubner-Richter, Max
Erwin von, 43, 45, 49
Schirach, Baldur von, 109,
112
Schönerer, Georg von, 24,
28, 29
Schulz, Walther, 49
Schutzstaffel. See SS
Seeckt, Hans von, 40, 46,
54, 60
Seisser, Hans von, 41
in Beer Hall Putsch, 42,
43, 46
Selzer, Michael, 21
Shimoni, Yehudah, 196
Shirer, William L., 19, 20,
36
Sicherheitdienst, (SD), 57,
189, 201
extermination camps and,
172
Siewierski (Polish
prosecutor), 176
Snyder, Louis L., 142, 177,
178
Soviet Union, German
invasion of, 58
Spandau Diary (Speer), 141
Speer, Albert, 15
becomes disillusioned with
Hitler, 133, 137
cooperation of, with
Americans, 134

during last weeks of war,
127
trial of, 138–41
Spielvogel, Jackson J., 24
SS (Schutzstaffel), 10, 11,
199
Himmler becomes head of,
90, 93
SS Association for Research
and Teaching on Heredity,
94
SS Einstaz, 189
Sternol, Maximilian, 183
Storm Troopers. See
Sturmabteilung
Strasser, Gregor, 67, 68, 92
Stresemann, Gustav, 39, 40
Stroessner, Alfredo, 186
Sturmabteilung (SA), 15,
38, 142
in Beer Hall Putsch, 41
Berlin mutiny of, 148
Röhm and creation of,
145–46

Taboada, Diogenes, 197
Thule Society, 33, 105
Todt, Fritz, 131
Treblinka, 172, 173
Twenty-Five Points, 34–35
22 Cells in Nuremberg
(Kelley), 76

United States, use of former
Nazis as spies for, 205
UXL, 199

Versailles, Treaty of, 12–13,
38
Victor, George, 19
Voelkische Freiheit

(newspaper), 63
völkisch nationalism, 29
  of German Workers' Party,
  33

Wagman, Robert J., 189,
  190
Wagner, Richard, 29–30
Wannsee Conference, 137,
  150
Warsaw ghetto, 172–73
Weimar Republic, 13
  chaotic condition of, 37

Nazi goal of overthrowing,
  38
Wiesenthal, Simon, 182,
  185, 187, 195
Willms, Regine, 201
World War I
  Germany's defeat in, stab-
  in-the-back theory and,
  32
  Göring in, 79–80
  Hess in, 104, 105

Zeppelin Stadium, 132